CONTENTS

INTRODUCTION

Why this Book?

I have put together this recipe book because I get asked all the time what my favorite restaurant dishes are. The pandemic is changing our world and the way we relate and do things. It's no longer business as usual and many people are now resorting to home cooking and homemade meals. However, some get sick missing out on their favorite Starbucks drink or Applebee's recipe, but it is what it is in the times we live in now.

Now, how about a recipe that looks like Applebee's Fiesta Lime Chicken with the scintillating copycat Paula Deen BBQ Sauce prepared right in the comfort of your home for your family and friends?

Wouldn't you like a recipe that tastes so much like Wendy's Strawberry Frosty, while still on track for ketosis? I bet you wish!

How does this Book make Weight Loss easier?

For many of us, the Keto diet is the best way to help us burn the fat, and to really get the flab off our bodies. But with the Keto diet, it can often be quite tricky. Since it does require you eat certain low carb foods and plenty of healthy fats, it's not something to easily come by with popular restaurant meals.

Yes, oftentimes, you might crave these recipes while still hoping to lose weight. Well, that's where this copycat cookbook comes in handy.

The Keto copycat recipe cookbook is for anyone who wants to lose weight, but doesn't want to miss out on classic restaurant flavors. It's really simple, when you prepare these combined with the Keto macros system, you're in for a treat. This book will give you just that.

If you're about starting the ketogenic diet, or already on it, Keto copycat recipes is the go-to cookbook for you to beat the crave. Keto Copycat Recipes is a collection of tested copycat recipes of the most popular restaurant dishes.

So, you do not have to worry about relying on conventional keto foods alone — with these recipes, you can still make delicious copycat meals that play nicely with your macros.

Below is a list of the most popular restaurant recipes adapted into the ketogenic diet. Enjoy!

BREAKFAST

IHOP Bacon Omelet

Serving: 2
Preparation time: 5 minutes; Cooking time: 10 minutes;
Nutritional Info: 736 Cal; 17.5 g Fats; 4.2 g Protein; 6.7 g Net Carb; 0 g Fiber;
Ingredients
- 12 slices of bacon, chopped, cooked
- 8 ounces American cheese
- ½ cup shredded Monterey Jack Cheese
- 8 eggs
- 4 tablespoons almond milk, divided

Directions
- Take a small pan, place it over medium heat and when hot, add American cheese in it, and then stir in 2 tablespoon milk.
- Cook until cheese melts and a smooth sauce comes together, stirring continuously, and when done, switch heat to the low level.
- Then take a medium bowl, crack the eggs in it, add 4 slices of bacon slices along with remaining milk and then whisk until well blended.
- Take a skillet pan, place it over medium heat, bring it to 350 degrees F, and then grease it with oil.
- Pour in prepared omelet batter in a rectangle shape and when they form up, pour one-fourth of the cooked cheese sauce over it.
- Roll the omelet in the form of a roll, top it with shredded Monterey Jack Cheese, and remaining chopped bacon.
- Transfer omelet to a plate and remaining with the remaining batter and cheese sauce.
- Serve each omelet with the remaining cheese sauce.

Starbucks Glazed Lemon Bread

Serving: 15
Preparation time: 10 minutes; Cooking time: 1 hour;
Nutritional Info: 121 Cal; 10 g Fats; 3 g Protein; 2 g Net Carb; 1 g Fiber;
Ingredients
For the bread:
- 1/2 cup and 2 tablespoons coconut flour
- 2 lemons, zested
- 1 ½ teaspoon baking powder
- ½ teaspoon salt
- 2/3 cup Monk fruit
- 9 tablespoons butter, unsalted, melted, cooled
- 4 teaspoons lemon juice
- 1 teaspoon vanilla extract, unsweetened
- 2 tablespoons cream cheese, softened
- 2 tablespoons heavy whipping cream
- 6 eggs

For the Glaze:
- 1 teaspoon lemon zest
- 2 tablespoons Monk fruit Powder
- 2 teaspoons lemon juice
- 2 tablespoons whipping cream

Directions
- Prepare the bread and for this, switch on the oven, then set it to 325 degrees F and let it preheat.
- Take a large bowl, crack the eggs in it, add baking powder, salt, vanilla, whipping cream, cream cheese, and monk fruit and then beat until well combined.
- Beat in flour, lemon zest, butter, and lemon juice until incorporated and then spoon the batter into a 9-by-5 inch bread pan lined with parchment paper.

- Bake the bread for 60 minutes until the top turn golden brown and then inserted a wooden skewer into the center of the bread comes out clean.
- When done, let the bread cool in the pan for 10 minutes.
- Meanwhile, prepare the glaze and for this, take a medium, place all of its ingredients in it and then whisk well until smooth.
- Lift out the bread from pan, spread the prepared glaze on top of bread, and then cut it into twelve slices.
- Serve straight away.

Garlic Cheddar Biscuit

Serving: 12

Preparation time: 10 minutes; Cooking time: 15 minutes;

Nutritional Info: 135 Cal; 11 g Fats; 5 g Protein; 1 g Net Carb; 1 g Fiber;

Ingredients

- 1/3 cup coconut flour
- 1 teaspoon minced garlic
- ¼ teaspoon salt
- 2 tablespoons sour cream
- ¼ teaspoon baking powder
- 1¼ teaspoons Italian seasoning
- 4½ tablespoons butter, unsalted, melted, cooled
- 1½ cup shredded cheddar cheese
- 4 eggs

Directions

- Switch on the oven, then set it to 400 degrees F and let it preheat.
- Meanwhile, take a large bowl, place butter in it, add salt, cream and eggs and then whisk until smooth.
- Whisk garlic, baking powder, Italian seasoning, and flour until incorporated and then fold in cheese until just mixed.
- Take a 12-cups muffin pan, grease it with oil, and then fill each cup with the prepared batter.
- Bake the biscuits for 15 minutes or more until the top turns golden brown.
- When done, let biscuits cool in the muffin pan for 10 minutes and then serve.

Starbucks Egg Bites with Cheese and Red Pepper

Serving: 3
Preparation time: 5 minutes; Cooking time: 10 minutes;
Nutritional Info: 286 Cal; 19.7 g Fats; 23.6 g Protein; 3.2 g Net Carb; 0.4 g Fiber;
Ingredients
- ¼ cup chopped roasted red pepper
- 1 green onion, chopped
- ¼ cup chopped spinach
- ¼ teaspoon salt
- ¼ teaspoon ground black pepper
- ¼ teaspoon hot sauce
- ½ cup cottage cheese
- 1 cup of water
- 4 eggs
- ½ cup shredded Monterey jack cheese

Directions
- Crack eggs in a food processor, add salt, black pepper, and both cheese and pulse for 1 minute until smooth.
- Tip the mixture into a large bowl, add spinach, pepper, and onion and then stir until combined.
- Take three silicone cups or ramekins, pour in prepared batter evenly, and then cover each mold with foil.
- Switch on the instant pot, pour water into the inner pot, insert a trivet stand, and then place prepared ramekins on top.
- Cover the pot with lid, make sure it is sealed, press the steam button, and let it cook for 10 minutes.
- When the instant pot, press the cancel button, let the pressure release naturally for 10 minutes, and then do quick pressure release.
- Carefully open the instant pot, remove the ramekins from it, cool then for 5 minutes, and then uncover them.
- Transfer egg bites to a plate and then serve.

Starbucks Bagels

Serving: 6
Preparation time: 10 minutes; Cooking time: 18 minutes;
Nutritional Info: 449 Cal; 35.5 g Fats; 27.8 g Protein; 6 g Net Carb; 4 g Fiber;
Ingredients
For the Bagels:
- 2 cups almond flour
- 1 teaspoon onion powder
- 1 teaspoon garlic powder
- 1 tablespoon baking powder
- 1 teaspoon Italian seasoning
- 3 cups shredded mozzarella cheese
- 3 eggs, divided
- 5 tablespoons cream cheese

For the Topping:
- 2/3 tablespoon sea salt
- 2 teaspoons onion powder
- 2 teaspoons garlic powder
- ¾ tablespoon poppy seeds
- 1 tablespoon sesame seeds

Directions
- Switch on the oven, then set it to 425 degrees F and let it preheat.
- Meanwhile, take a baking sheet, line it with parchment paper, and then set aside until required.
- Take a large bowl, place flour in it, add onion powder, garlic powder, Italian seasoning, and baking powder and then stir until well combined.
- Prepare the egg wash and for this, take a small bowl, crack an egg in it, whisk well, and then set aside.

- Take a medium heatproof bowl, place cream cheese and mozzarella in it, microwave for 1 minute and 30 seconds, stir until mixed, continue microwaving for another minute and then stir until well combined.
- Take a separate large bowl, crack the remaining eggs in it, add flour mixture and then whisk well by using an electric beater until incorporated and the dough comes together.
- Divide the prepared dough evenly into six pieces, roll each piece into a ball, press a thumb or finger in its center and then shape it like a bagel.
- Repeat with the remaining pieces and arrange bagels onto the prepared baking sheet.
- Take a small bowl, place all the ingredients for the topping in it and then stir until mixed.
- Brush the prepared egg wash on top of each bagel, sprinkle with the prepared topping seasoning and then bake for 13 to 15 minutes until golden brown.
- Serve straight away.

MCGriddle Bacon Sandwiches

Serving: 2
Preparation time: 15 minutes; Cooking time: 25 minutes;
Nutritional Info: 374 Cal; 29 g Fats; 19 g Protein; 2 g Net Carb; 4 g Fiber;
Ingredients
For the Buns:
- 1 cup almond flour
- 2 teaspoons baking powder
- ½ teaspoon liquid stevia
- 1 ½ teaspoon erythritol sweetener
- 1 ½ teaspoon vanilla extract, unsweetened
- ½ cup pancake syrup, low-carb, sugar-free
- 3 ounces cream cheese, softened
- 3 eggs

For the Filling:
- 6 slices of bacon, cooked
- ½ teaspoon salt
- ½ teaspoon ground black pepper
- 6 slices of cheese
- 6 eggs

Directions
- Take a small saucepan, place it over medium-high heat, add pancake syrup, and bring it to a boil.
- Continue boiling the syrup for 4 to 8 minutes until reduced by half and thickened, stirring continuously, then spread the syrup on the baking pan lined with parchment paper and let it freeze for 1 hour.
- Then switch on the oven, set it to 350 degrees F and let it preheat.
- Prepare the buns and for this, place all of its remaining ingredients into a blender and then pulse for 2 minutes until smooth.

- Take a large cookie sheet, line it with a foil, place 12 rings of jars, grease their insides with oil and then evenly pour the blended batter for buns in them, 3 tablespoons per ring.
- Remove the frozen syrup from the freezer, peel the parchment sheet, then cut syrup into small pieces and evenly distribute them into the batter in the rings.
- Place the cookie sheet into the oven, bake for 15 minutes until batter for buns has set, and when done, let them cool in the cookie sheet for 5 minutes and then remove buns from the rings to cool completely.
- Meanwhile, prepare the filling for the buns, and for this, fry the eggs until cooked to the desired level and cook the bacon slices until crisp.
- Assemble the sandwiches and for this, top each bun with a slice of bacon, a fried egg, a cheese slice, and then cover the top with another bun.
- Serve straight away.

Kind Bars

Serving: 12
Preparation time: 5 minutes; Cooking time: 5 minutes;
Nutritional Info: 216 Cal; 18 g Fats; 8 g Protein; 3 g Net Carb; 4 g Fiber;
Ingredients
- 2 cups whole almonds, unsalted
- 2 tablespoons hemp seeds
- ½ cup pumpkin seeds, unsalted
- 2 medium vanilla bean
- 1/3 cup coconut flakes, unsweetened
- ½ teaspoon of sea salt
- ¼ cup erythritol sweetener
- ¼ cup liquid stevia
- 2 teaspoons vanilla extract, unsweetened
- ¼ cup almond butter

Directions
- Take a large bowl, place almond, hemp seeds, pumpkin seeds, and coconut flakes in it and then stir until mixed, set aside until required.
- Take a large saucepan, place it over medium heat, add salt, erythritol, stevia, and butter, and cook for 3 to 5 minutes until smooth, stirring frequently.
- Remove pan from heat, add vanilla beans and extract, stir until mixed, then spoon the mixture into the almond mixture and stir until combined.
- Take 8-by-8 inches baking pan, line it with parchment paper, spoon almond mixture in it, spread it evenly by pressing it down, and smooth the top.
- Cool the almond mixture at room temperature and, when cooled, lift the parchment sheet to transfer the granola to a cutting board and then cut it into bars.
- Serve straight away.

Cracker Barrel Hashbrown Casserole

Serving: 4

Preparation time: 5 minutes; Cooking time: 10 minutes;

Nutritional Info: 271 Cal; 26 g Fats; 5 g Protein; 2.9 g Net Carb; 0.1 g Fiber;

Ingredients

- 1 ½ cups shredded cauliflower stalks
- ½ tablespoon onion powder
- ½ teaspoon salt
- ½ teaspoon ground black pepper
- ½ tablespoon bouillon powder
- ½ cup sour cream
- ½ cup shredded cheddar cheese and Monterey jack cheese, divided
- ¼ cup mayonnaise
- 2 tablespoons butter, unsalted

Directions

- Switch on the oven, then set it to 350 degrees F and let it preheat.
- Reserve 1/3 cup of the cheese mixture, add remaining cheese into a large bowl and then add remaining ingredients.
- Stir until mixed, take an 8-by-8 inch baking dish, grease it with oil and spread prepared mixture in it.
- Top the mixture with reserved cheese and then bake for 60 minutes until bubbly and the top turns golden.
- Serve straight away.

Starbucks Sous Vide Egg Bites

Serving: 4

Preparation time: 5 minutes; Cooking time: 8 minutes;

Nutritional Info: 258.8 Cal; 19.6 g Fats; 18.1 g Protein; 2.6 g Net Carb; 0 g Fiber;

Ingredients

- 4 strips of bacon, cooked, chopped
- ½ teaspoon salt
- ¼ teaspoon hot sauce
- ½ cup cottage cheese
- 4 eggs
- ¾ cup shredded mozzarella cheese
- ¼ cup heavy cream
- 1 cup of water

Directions

- Crack eggs in a food processor, add salt, hot sauce, cream, and both cheeses and pulse for 1 minute until smooth.
- Take four silicon molds, distribute chopped bacon in them, evenly pour in egg batter, and then cover each mold with foil.
- Switch on the instant pot, pour water into the inner pot, insert a trivet stand, and then place prepared ramekins on top.
- Cover the pot with lid, make sure it is sealed, press the steam button, and let it cook for 8 minutes.
- When the instant pot, press the cancel button, let the pressure release naturally for 10 minutes, and then do quick pressure release.
- Carefully open the instant pot, remove the ramekins from it, cool then for 5 minutes, and then uncover them.
- Transfer egg bites to a plate and then serve.

Sausage and Egg Breakfast Sandwich

Serving: 2

Preparation time: 5 minutes; Cooking time: 5 minutes;

Nutritional Info: 880 Cal; 82 g Fats; 32 g Protein; 6 g Net Carb; 2 g Fiber;

Ingredients

- 4 sausage patties, cooked
- 6 slices of avocado
- 2 tablespoons mayonnaise
- 2 tablespoons butter, unsalted
- 4 slices of cheddar cheese
- 4 eggs

Directions

- Take a large skillet pan, place it over medium heat, add butter, and then place flour egg molds or rings of mason jars in it.
- Crack an egg into each mold, break the yolks and whisk the egg by using a fork, then cover the pan with a lid and cook for 3 to 4 minutes until the egg has thoroughly cooked.
- Assemble the sandwich for this, place an egg onto a plate, spread 1 tablespoon of mayonnaise on top, top with one patty of sausage, a cheese slice, and three avocado slices and then cover the top with another egg.
- Repeat to make another sandwich and then serve.

Egg Roll in a Bowl

Serving: 2

Preparation time: 10 minutes; Cooking time: 15 minutes;

Nutritional Info: 355 Cal; 30 g Fats; 16 g Protein; 3 g Net Carb; 1 g Fiber;

Ingredients

- ½ pound spicy bulk pork sausage
- 1 cups shredded green cabbage
- 2/3 tablespoon chopped green onions
- 1/8 teaspoon garlic powder
- 1/8 tablespoon minced ginger
- 1/3 teaspoon salt
- 1/3 teaspoon ground black pepper
- 1/3 tablespoon rice vinegar
- 2/3 tablespoon tamari
- 1 ¼ tablespoon water
- 2/3 tablespoon toasted sesame oil
- 1/3 tablespoon toasted sesame seeds

Directions

- Take a large skillet pan, place it over medium-high heat and when hot, add sausage, break it up and then cook for 5 to 6 minutes until nicely browned.
- Drain the excess grease from the pan, stir in water to remove browned bits from the bottom of the pan, then switch heat to medium level and add green onion and cabbage in it.
- Add ginger, garlic powder and sesame oil, season with salt and black pepper, and then cook for 5 minutes or more until the vegetables have softened.
- Stir in tamari and vinegar, continue cooking for 2 minutes until hot and then remove the pan from heat.
- Distribute sausage and vegetable mixture between two bowls, sprinkle with sesame seeds and then serve.

Orange Julius

Serving: 2

Preparation time: 5 minutes; Cooking time: 0 minutes;

Nutritional Info: 325 Cal; 34 g Fats; 3 g Protein; 2.5 g Net Carb; 0 g Fiber;

Ingredients

- 2/3 cup heavy whipping cream
- 3 tablespoons erythritol sweetener
- 1 ½ teaspoon lemon juice
- 1 ½ teaspoons orange extract, unsweetened
- 2 tablespoons cream cheese
- 1 ½ cups crushed ice

Directions

- Plugin a high-powdered blender, pour in the cream, and then pulse for a minute until churned.
- Add remaining ingredients and continue blending for another minute until smooth.
- Divide the orange Julius between two glasses and then serve immediately.

Shamrock Shake

Serving: 2

Preparation time: 5 minutes; Cooking time: 0 minutes;

Nutritional Info: 354 Cal; 31.5 g Fats; 2.8 g Protein; 6.8 g Net Carb; 1 g Fiber;

Ingredients

- 2/3 cup almond milk, unsweetened
- 4 small scoops of vanilla ice cream, low carb
- 2 teaspoons spinach powder
- ¼ teaspoon mint extract, unsweetened

Directions

- Add all the ingredients in the order into a food processor, shut with the lid, and then pulse for 1 minute until smooth.
- Divide the shake evenly between two glasses and then serve.

Strawberries and Cream Smoothie

Serving: 2

Preparation time: 5 minutes; Cooking time: 0 minutes;

Nutritional Info: 213.5 Cal; 18.7 g Fats; 2.1 g Protein; 5.5 g Net Carb; 3.6 g Fiber;

Ingredients

- 1 ½ cup cashew milk, unsweetened
- 24-ounces coconut milk, unsweetened
- 2 teaspoons lemon juice
- 1 teaspoon vanilla extract, unsweetened
- 1 teaspoon salt, divided
- 2 tablespoons erythritol sweetener
- 2 cups whole fresh strawberries, halved
- 2 tablespoons avocado oil
- 1 cup of ice cubes

Directions

- Add all the ingredients in the order into a food processor, shut with the lid, and then pulse for 1 minute until smooth.
- Divide the smoothie evenly between two glasses and then serve.

LUNCH – BEEF RECIPES

Wendy's Chili

Serving: 8
Preparation time: 10 minutes; Cooking time: 1 hour and 50 minutes;
Nutritional Info: 344 Cal; 21 g Fats; 27 g Protein; 9 g Net Carb; 2 g Fiber;
Ingredients
- 3 pounds ground beef
- 1 ½ cups diced white onion
- ½ cup diced red bell pepper
- 1 cup chopped tomatoes
- 2/3 cups diced celery
- ½ cup diced green bell pepper
- 1 teaspoon garlic powder
- 1 teaspoon salt
- 2 teaspoons erythritol sweetener
- 1 teaspoon cumin
- ½ teaspoon ground black pepper
- ½ teaspoon oregano
- 3 tablespoons red chili powder
- 1 ½ teaspoon Worcestershire sauce
- 15 ounces crushed tomatoes
- 1 ½ cups tomato juice
- 2 tablespoons avocado oil

Directions
- Take a large pot, place it over medium heat, add oil and when hot, add beef and then cook for 10 to 15 minutes until golden brown.
- Drain the excess greases, add bell peppers, tomatoes, celery, and onion, switch heat to medium-high level and cook for 5 minutes.
- Add remaining ingredients, stir until well mixed and then simmer the chili for 1 hour and 30 minutes until cooked, covering the pot.
- Serve straight away.

Olive Garden's Zuppa Toscana Soup

Serving: 6

Preparation time: 5 minutes; Cooking time: 40 minutes;

Nutritional Info: 450 Cal; 37 g Fats; 18 g Protein; 12 g Net Carb; 3 g Fiber;

Ingredients

- 1 large head of cauliflower, cut into florets
- 1 pound sausage
- 3 cups kale leaves, chopped
- 1 medium white onion, peeled, chopped
- 1 ½ tablespoon minced garlic
- ½ teaspoon salt
- ½ teaspoon red pepper flakes
- ¼ teaspoon ground black pepper
- 4 cups of water
- 16 ounces chicken broth
- 1 cup heavy cream

Directions

- Take a large pot, place it over medium-high heat and when hot, add sausage, crumble it, and then cook for 10 to 15 minutes until brown.
- Add garlic and onion, stir until mixed, cook for 5 minutes, and then season salt, black pepper, and red pepper.
- Switch heat to medium level, add florets, pour in water and chicken broth, stir and then cook for 20 minutes until florets have turned tender.
- Then switch heat to the low level, add kale, pour in the cream, stir until combined, and then remove the pot from heat.
- Ladle soup among six bowls and then serve.

In N' Out Burger

Serving: 5   Preparation time: 10 minutes; Cooking time: 10 minutes;

Nutritional Info: 696 Cal; 49.5 g Fats; 52.2 g Protein; 6.5 g Net Carb; 4 g Fiber;

Ingredients

For the Patties:

- 1 ½ pound ground beef
- 1 ½ teaspoon salt
- 1 teaspoon ground black pepper
- 5 slices of American cheese

For the Sauce:

- 1/3 cup mayonnaise
- 1 tablespoon ketchup, sugar-free
- 1 teaspoon mustard paste
- 2 tablespoons diced pickles
- 2 teaspoons pickle juice
- ½ teaspoon salt
- ½ teaspoon paprika
- ½ teaspoon garlic powder

For the Toppings:

- 10 slices of tomato
- 20 lettuce leaves
- ½ of large white onion, peeled, sliced thin
- 10 pickles slices

Directions

Prepare the sauce and for this, take a small bowl, place all of its ingredients in it, whisk until mixed; set aside until required.

Prepare the patties and for this, take a medium bowl, place beef in it, add salt and black pepper, stir until well combined, and then shape the mixture into ten balls.

Take a griddle pan, place it over high heat, grease it with oil and when hot, place meatball on it, press them down, and then cook 4 to 5 minutes per side until thoroughly cooked and browned.

When done, place a cheese slice on top of one patty, stack with another patty, and repeat with the remaining patties.

Assemble the burgers and for this, use two lettuce leaves as the bottom part of the bun, add some slices on onion, top with stacked burger patties, and then top with two slices of each tomato and pickles.

Drizzle the prepared sauce over patties, and then cover the top with two lettuce leaves.Assemble the remaining burgers in the same manner and then serve.

Big Mac Bites

Serving: 16
Preparation time: 15 minutes; Cooking time: 15 minutes;
Nutritional Info: 182 Cal; 12 g Fats; 10 g Protein; 0.6 g Net Carb; 0.4 g Fiber;
Ingredients
For the Bites:

- ¼ cup diced white onion
- 1½ pounds ground beef
- 1 teaspoon salt
- 16 slices dill pickle
- 4 slices of American cheese
- 16 leaves of lettuce

For the Sauce:

- 4 tablespoon dill pickle relish
- 1 teaspoon onion powder
- 1 teaspoon garlic powder
- 1 teaspoon paprika
- 1 teaspoon white wine vinegar
- 2 tablespoon mustard paste
- ½ cup mayonnaise

Directions

- Switch on the oven, then set it to 400 degrees F and let it preheat.
- Meanwhile, prepare the bites and for this, take a large bowl, place beef in it, add onion and salt and then stir until well combined.
- Shape the mixture into sixteen balls and then press down slightly to flatten balls into patties.
- Arrange the patties into a large baking sheet lined with parchment sheet and then bake for 15 minutes until thoroughly cooked, turning halfway.
- Meanwhile, prepare the sauce and for this, take a medium bowl, place all of its ingredients in it and then whisk until combined.

- When patties have baked, remove the baking sheet from the oven and then drain the excess grease.
- Assemble the bites and for this, cut each slice of American cheese into four squares, place each cheese square on top of each patty, return the baking sheet into the oven and wait until cheese melts.
- Meanwhile, cut lettuce into squares and when the cheese melts, top each patty with lettuce squares and a slice of pickle and then secure the bite by inserting a skewer through it.
- Serve the bite with prepared sauce.

McDonalds' Sausage Sandwich

Serving: 5

Preparation time: 10 minutes; Cooking time: 25 minutes;

Nutritional Info: 362 Cal; 31 g Fats; 18 g Protein; 3 g Net Carb; 1 g Fiber;

Ingredients

For the Buns:

- 1 ½ cups almond flour
- ¼ teaspoon salt
- 1 ¼ teaspoons baking soda
- 1 tablespoon erythritol sweetener
- 2 tablespoons liquid stevia
- 1 teaspoon vanilla extract, unsweetened
- 2 tablespoons butter, unsalted
- 4 tablespoons cream cheese
- 3 eggs

For the Filling:

- 5 cooked sausage patties
- 5 eggs, fried
- 5 slices of provolone cheese

Directions

- Switch on a mini-waffle iron, then set it to high heat setting and let it preheat.
- Prepare the buns and for this, place all of its ingredients into a large bowl and then beat by using an electric beater until smooth batter comes together.
- Then ladle 2 tablespoons of waffle batter into the waffle iron, shut with the lid, and then cook for 3 to 5 minutes until golden brown and hard.
- Transfer the waffle to a plate and then repeat with the remaining batter; you will get ten waffles.
- While waffles cook, fry the eggs to the desired level and cook the sausage patties until golden brown on both sides.
- Assemble the sandwich and for this, take a waffle, place a patty on it, top with a fried egg and a slice of cheese, and then cover the top with another waffle.
- Prepare remaining sandwiches in the same manner and then serve.

LUNCH – POULTRY RECIPES

Longhorn's Parmesan Crusted Chicken

Serving: 4

Preparation time: 10 minutes; Cooking time: 30 minutes;

Nutritional Info: 557 Cal; 42 g Fats; 31 g Protein; 10 g Net Carb; 2 g Fiber;

Ingredients

- 4 chicken breasts, skinless
- 2 teaspoons salt
- 2 teaspoons ground black pepper
- 2 tablespoons avocado oil

For the Marinade:

- 1 tablespoon minced garlic
- ½ teaspoon ground black pepper
- 1 teaspoon lemon juice
- 3 tablespoon Worcestershire sauce
- 1 teaspoon white vinegar
- ½ cup avocado oil
- ½ cup ranch dressing

For the Parmesan Crust:

- 1 cup panko breadcrumbs
- 6 ounces parmesan cheese, chopped
- 5 tablespoons melted butter, unsalted
- 6 ounces provolone cheese, chopped
- 2 teaspoons garlic powder
- 6 tablespoons ranch salad dressing, low-carb

Directions

- Prepare the marinade and for this, take a small bowl, place all of its ingredients in it and then whisk until well combined.

- Pound each chicken until ¾-inch thick, then season with salt and black pepper and transfer chicken pieces to a large plastic bag.
- Pour in the prepared marinade, seal the bag, turn it upside to coat chicken with it and let it rest for a minimum of 30 minutes in the refrigerator.
- Then take a large skillet pan, place it over medium-high heat, add oil and when hot, place marinated chicken breast in it and then cook for 5 minutes per side until chicken is no longer pink and nicely seared on all sides.
- Transfer chicken to a plate and repeat with the remaining chicken pieces.
- Meanwhile, switch on the oven, set it to 450 degrees F, and let it preheat.
- When the chicken has cooked, prepare the parmesan crust and for this, take a small heatproof bowl, place both cheeses in it, pour in ranch dressing and milk, stir until mixed, and then microwave for 30 seconds.
- Then stir the cheese mixture again until smooth and continue microwaving for another 15 seconds.
- Stir the cheese mixture again, spread evenly on top of each chicken breast, arrange them in a baking sheet and then bake for 5 minutes until cheese has melted.
- Meanwhile, take a small bowl, place breadcrumbs in it, stir in garlic powder and butter in it.
- After 5 minutes of baking, spread the breadcrumbs mixture on top of the chicken and then continue baking for 2 minutes until the panko mixture turns light brown.
- Serve chicken straight away with cauliflower mashed potatoes.

Teriyaki Wings

Serving: 6

Preparation time: 15 minutes; Cooking time: 1 hour and 15 minutes;

Nutritional Info: 324 Cal; 21 g Fats; 27 g Protein; 2 g Net Carb; 1 g Fiber;

Ingredients

For The Wings:

- 2 pounds chicken wings,
- 2 tablespoons baking powder
- 1 teaspoon of sea salt

For The Sauce:

- 2 tablespoons erythritol confectioners
- 1 tablespoon minced garlic
- 1 teaspoon grated ginger
- 1 teaspoon xanthan gum
- 1 tablespoon apple cider vinegar
- ¼ cup coconut aminos
- ½ teaspoon avocado oil
- ½ cup water, divided

For The Garnish:

- 2 teaspoons sesame seeds
- 2 chives, chopped

Directions

- Prepare the chicken wings and for this, take a large baking sheet, line it with paper towels, spread chicken wings on it and let them rest for 20 minutes until paper towels have soaked excess moisture.
- Meanwhile, switch on the oven, set it to 250 degrees F, then set the baking rack to middle-lower position and let it preheat.
- After 20 minutes, transfer the chicken wings into large plastic bags, add a baking sheet, seal the bag, and then turn it upside down until the chicken wings are coated evenly.

- Spread chicken wings in a single layer on a baking sheet lined with foil and then bake for 30 minutes.
- Then switch the temperature of the oven to 425 degrees F, place the baking sheet to the top-middle rack of the oven and continue baking for 45 minutes, turning halfway through.
- Meanwhile, prepare the sauce and for this, take a medium saucepan, place it over medium-high heat, pour in ¼ cup water, and then whisk in the garlic, ginger, sweetener, vinegar, and coconut aminos until combined.
- Take a small bowl, pour in the remaining water, add xanthan gum and oil and then whisk until combined.
- Pour the oil mixture into the pan and cook for 5 to 8 minutes until sauce has thickened, whisking constantly.
- When done, pour the sauce into a large bowl and then set aside until required.
- When the chicken wings have baked, let them rest in the pan for 5 minutes, then transfer them into the bowl containing sauce and toss until coated.
- Sprinkle sesame seeds and chives on chicken wings and then serve.

Panda Express Kung Pao Chicken

Serving: 10
Preparation time: 10 minutes; Cooking time: 30 minutes;
Nutritional Info: 295 Cal; 16.4 g Fats; 31.7 g Protein; 3.2 g Net Carb; 2 g Fiber;
Ingredients

- 35 ounces chicken thighs, skinless, ½-inch cubed
- 14 ounces zucchini, destemmed, ½-inch diced
- 14 ounces red bell pepper, cored, 1-inch cubed
- 1 green onion, sliced
- 15 pieces of dried Chinese red peppers
- 1 ½ teaspoons minced garlic
- 1 teaspoon minced ginger
- 3 ounces roasted peanuts
- ¼ teaspoon ground black pepper
- ¼ teaspoon xanthan gum
- 3 tablespoons coconut oil
- 1 tablespoon balsamic vinegar
- 1 tablespoon chili garlic sauce
- ¾ tablespoon sesame oil

For the Marinade:

- 3 tablespoons coconut aminos
- 1 tablespoon coconut oil

For the Sauce:

- 3 tablespoons monk fruit sweetener
- 3 tablespoons coconut aminos

Directions

- Marinade the chicken and for this, take a large bowl, place the chicken pieces in it, and then add all the ingredients for the marinade in it.
- Stir until chicken is well coated and then marinate for a minimum of 30 minutes in the refrigerator.

- Then take a large skillet pan, add 1 tablespoon of coconut oil in it and when it melted, add marinated chicken and cook for 10 minutes or more until it starts to release its water.
- After 10 minutes, push the chicken to the sides of the pan to create a well in its middle, slowly stir in xanthan gum into the water released by chicken and cook for 2 to 4 minutes until it starts to thicken.
- Then stir chicken into the thicken liquid and continue cooking for 10 minutes or more until chicken has thoroughly cooked, set aside until required.
- Return pan over medium-high heat, add 1 tablespoon oil, and when it melts, add bell pepper and zucchini cubes and then cook for 5 to 8 minutes until lightly browned.
- Transfer vegetables to a separate plate, then add remaining coconut oil into the pan, add Chinese red peppers, ginger, garlic, vinegar, and chili garlic sauce.
- Stir until mixed, cook for 3 minutes, add ingredients for the sauce along with peanuts, green onion, black pepper, and sesame oil and continue cooking for 3 minutes, stirring frequently.
- Return chicken and vegetables into the pan, toss until well mixed and then continue cooking for 3 to 5 minutes until hot.
- Serve straight away.

Butter Chicken

Serving: 6

Preparation time: 10 minutes; Cooking time: 20 minutes;

Nutritional Info: 293 Cal; 17 g Fats; 29 g Protein; 6 g Net Carb; 3 g Fiber;

Ingredients

- 1 ½ pounds chicken breast, cubed
- 3 teaspoons grated ginger
- 3 teaspoons minced garlic
- 2 tablespoons garam masala
- 1 tablespoon coconut oil
- 4 ounces almond yogurt

For the Sauce:

- 1 large white onion, peeled, quarter
- 2 teaspoons grated ginger
- 14.5 ounces crushed tomatoes
- 2 teaspoons minced garlic
- 1 ½ teaspoon salt
- 1 teaspoon red chili powder
- 1 tablespoon ground coriander
- 2 teaspoons cumin
- ½ tablespoon garam masala
- 2 tablespoons butter, unsalted
- ½ cup heavy cream

Directions

- Cut the chicken breast into 2-inch cubes, place them into a large bowl, add 1 teaspoon each of ginger and garlic along with garam masala and yogurt and then stir until well combined.
- Place the chicken into the refrigerator and let it marinate for a minimum of 30 minutes.

- Meanwhile, prepare the sauce and for this, place onion pieces in the blender, add tomatoes, garlic, ginger, and all the spices and then pulse for 2 to 3 minutes until smooth.
- When the chicken has marinated, take a large skillet pan, place it over medium-high heat, add oil and when it melts, add marinated chicken pieces and cook for 4 minutes per side until nicely browned.
- Then pour in the sauce, cook for 6 minutes, add butter and cream and stir until well mixed.
- Cook the chicken for another mixture, season with salt, and then remove the pan from heat.
- Garnish the butter chicken with cilantro and then serve.

Chang's Lettuce Wraps

Serving: 8
Preparation time: 10 minutes; Cooking time: 15 minutes;
Nutritional Info: 149 Cal; 9 g Fats; 12 g Protein; 2.5 g Net Carb; 2 g Fiber;
Ingredients
For the Sauce:
- 1 tablespoon minced garlic
- ½ teaspoon grated ginger
- 1 tablespoon Swerve sweetener
- 3 tablespoons soy sauce
- 1 tablespoon apple cider vinegar
- 1 tablespoon almond butter
- 1 tablespoon sesame oil

For the Wraps:
- 1 pound ground chicken
- 3 ounces chopped shiitake mushrooms
- 3 green onions, sliced
- 2 teaspoons onion powder
- ½ cup diced jicama
- ¼ teaspoon salt
- ¼ teaspoon ground black pepper
- 1 tablespoon avocado oil
- 1 large head of butter lettuce

Directions
- Prepare the sauce and for this, take a medium bowl, place all of its ingredients in it and then whisk until combined, set aside until required.
- Take a large skillet pan, place it over medium heat, add oil and when hot, add ground chicken, crumble it and then cook for 5 to 8 minutes until no longer pink.
- Season chicken with onion powder, salt, and black pepper, add mushrooms, green onion, and jicama and then cook for 5 minutes until mushrooms have turned softened.
- Pour in the prepared sauce, stir until combined, cook for 2 minutes until hot, and then remove the pan from heat.
- Divide lettuce leaves into sixteen portions, top each with ¼ cup of the chicken and then serve straight away.

Asian Chicken Taco Lettuce Wraps

Serving: 4

Preparation time: 15 minutes; Cooking time: 20 minutes;

Nutritional Info: 161 Cal; 9.1 g Fats; 14.5 g Protein; 4.9 g Net Carb; 1.2 g Fiber;

Ingredients

For the Chicken:

- 1 tablespoon minced garlic
- 1 pound chicken thighs, skinless, boneless
- 2 tablespoons taco seasoning
- 1 tablespoon avocado oil

For the Wrap:

- 1 large avocado, peeled, pitted, diced
- ¼ cup diced white onion
- 8 leaves of romaine lettuce
- 1 medium tomato, diced

For the Cilantro Sauce:

- 1 jalapeno pepper
- ½ teaspoon minced garlic
- ½ cup cilantro leaves
- ½ of lime, juiced
- ¼ teaspoon salt
- ½ cup sour cream
- 2 tablespoons avocado oil

Directions

- Prepare the chicken and for this, place chicken in a large plastic bag, add remaining ingredients in it, seal the bag and shake well until chicken is well coated.
- Place the bag into the refrigerator and then let it marinate for a minimum of 30 minutes.

- Then take a griddle pan, place it over medium-high heat, grease it with oil and when hot, place marinated chicken on it and cook for 10 minutes per side until cooked and nicely browned.
- While chicken marinates, prepare the cilantro sauce and for this, place all of its ingredients in a food processor and then pulse for 1 minute until blended; set aside until required.
- Assemble the wraps and for this, distribute chicken among lettuce leaves, then top with onion, avocado and tomatoes, and drizzle with prepared cilantro sauce.
- Serve straight away.

KFC Fried Chicken

Serving: 6

Preparation time: 15 minutes; Cooking time: 18 minutes;

Nutritional Info: 590.2 Cal; 39.6 g Fats; 57.6 g Protein; 1.1 g Net Carb; 1 g Fiber;

Ingredients

For the Seasoning:

- 1 teaspoon celery salt
- 1 teaspoon of sea salt
- 1 teaspoon ginger powder
- 1 tablespoon ground white pepper
- 2 teaspoons garlic salt
- 1 teaspoon ground black pepper
- 4 teaspoons paprika
- ¼ teaspoon dried oregano
- ½ teaspoon dried thyme
- 1 teaspoon mustard powder

For the Marinade:

- ½ of the seasoning
- 4 tablespoons white vinegar
- 3 tablespoons heavy cream
- 2 cups almond milk, unsweetened
- 2 eggs

For the Chicken:

- 8 ½ cups avocado oil
- 2 pounds of chicken drumsticks
- 2 ½ cups whey protein powder

Directions

- Prepare the seasoning and for this, take a small bowl, place all of its ingredients in it and then stir until mixed, set aside until required.

- Prepare the marinade and for this, take a large bowl, pour in milk, add vinegar and cream, whisk until blended and then let it sit for 10 minutes.
- Then whisk in eggs until combined, and whisk in ½ of seasoning until smooth.
- Place chicken pieces into a large plastic bag, pour in the marinade, seal the bag, turn it upside down to coat chicken and then let it marinate in the refrigerator for a minimum of 4 hours.
- Cook the chicken, and for this, take a large pan, place it over medium heat, pour in the oil, and heat it for 12 minutes or more until the temperature reaches 325 degrees F.
- Spread remaining seasoning mixture on a plate, take a chicken piece, coat it with the seasoning mix and then add into the pan.
- Add more seasoned chicken pieces into the pan until filled and cook for 16 to 18 minutes until the internal temperature of chicken reaches 165 degrees F and turns nicely browned, turning chicken frequently.
- When done, transfer fried chicken to a plate lined with paper towels, and then repeat with the remaining chicken pieces.
- Serve straight away.

Buffalo Wings

Serving: 3

Preparation time: 10 minutes; Cooking time: 45 minutes;

Nutritional Info: 391 Cal; 32 g Fats; 31 g Protein; 1 g Net Carb; 0 g Fiber;

Ingredients

- 12 chicken wings, frozen
- 1/2 teaspoon salt
- ¼ teaspoon ground black pepper
- ½ cup avocado oil

For the Sauce:

- ½ tablespoon minced garlic
- ¼ teaspoon paprika
- ¼ teaspoon cayenne pepper
- 4 tablespoons butter, salted
- ¼ cup hot sauce, low-carb

Directions

- Switch on the oven, then set it to 400 degrees F and let it preheat.
- Meanwhile, take a large baking dish, spread chicken wings on it, rub them with oil, and then sprinkle with salt and black pepper.
- Bake the chicken wings for 45 minutes until crisp, turning halfway through.
- Meanwhile, prepare the sauce and for this, take a small saucepan, place it over medium-low heat, add butter and garlic and cook for 3 to 5 minutes until butter melts.
- Add remaining ingredients for the sauce, whisk until combined, cook for 2 minutes until hot, and then remove pan from heat.
- Add baked chicken wings into the sauce and then toss until well coated.
- Serve straight away.

Chicken Fried Rice

Serving: 4

Preparation time: 10 minutes; Cooking time: 15 minutes;

Nutritional Info: 324 Cal; 19 g Fats; 32 g Protein; 2.8 g Net Carb; 3 g Fiber;

Ingredients

- 2 cups riced cauliflower, frozen
- 1 large green onion, sliced
- 1 pound chicken breast, skinless, ½-inch cubed
- ¼ cup frozen peas
- 1 ½ teaspoon salt
- 1 teaspoon ground black pepper
- ½ teaspoon garlic powder
- 1 teaspoon grated ginger
- 2 teaspoons erythritol sweetener
- ½ teaspoon crushed red pepper flakes
- 3 tablespoons butter, unsalted, divided
- 3 tablespoons coconut aminos
- 2 eggs, beaten
- 2 tablespoons toasted sesame oil

Directions

- Take a large skillet pan, place it over medium-high heat, add 1 tablespoon butter and when it melts, add beaten eggs, season with 1/3 teaspoon salt, and ¼ teaspoon black pepper and then cook for 2 minutes until thoroughly cooked.
- Transfer eggs to a plate, add 1 tablespoon butter into the pan, and when it melted, add chicken pieces.
- Add half of each garlic, ginger, and red pepper flakes, season ½ teaspoon each of salt and black pepper, and then cook for 6 minutes until thoroughly cooked.
- Transfer chicken to a plate, then add 1 tablespoon butter into the pan and when it melts, add peas, cauliflower, and green onion, and then add remaining garlic, ginger, and red pepper flakes.

- Season with remaining salt and black pepper, cook for 5 minutes until vegetables have thoroughly heated and tender, and then stir in sesame oil and soy sauce.
- Return the chicken and eggs into the pan, toss until mixed, and then cook for 2 minutes until hot.
- Garnish rice and chicken with some more green onion and then serve.

Tso's Shrimp and Broccoli

Serving: 4
Preparation time: 5 minutes; Cooking time: 20 minutes;
Nutritional Info: 443 Cal; 18 g Fats; 54 g Protein; 2 g Net Carb; 2 g Fiber;
Ingredients

- 1 large head of broccoli, cut into florets
- 1 pound medium shrimp, tails removed, peeled, deveined
- ½ tablespoon minced garlic
- 1 teaspoon of sea salt
- ½ teaspoon ground black pepper
- 1 tablespoon crushed red pepper
- 2 tablespoons monk fruit sweetener
- 2 tablespoons white vinegar
- 3 tablespoons liquid aminos
- 2 tablespoons avocado oil
- 1/3 cup ketchup, sugar-free
- 1 teaspoon toasted sesame seeds

Directions

- Take a large bowl, place broccoli florets in it, cover with a plastic wrap, microwave for 10 minutes or more until florets have steamed, and then drain them well.
- Meanwhile, take a medium bowl, place the shrimps in it and then season with salt and black pepper.
- Prepare the sauce and for this, take a small saucepan, place it over medium heat, add garlic, sweetener, ketchup, soy sauce, and vinegar and then stir until mixed.
- Bring the mixture to a boil and then remove the pan from heat.
- Take a large skillet pan, place it over medium-high heat, add oil and when hot, add seasoned shrimps, and then cook for 5 to 8 minutes until turned pink.
- Drizzle with sauce, toss well until coated, and stir-fry for 3 to 5 minutes until shrimps have caramelized slightly.
- When done, remove the pan from heat and garnish shrimps with sesame seeds.
- Distribute the broccoli florets among four plates, top with shrimps, and then serve.

LUNCH – FISH AND SEAFOOD RECIPES

Red Lobster's Shrimp Scampi

Serving: 4

Preparation time: 5 minutes; Cooking time: 10 minutes;

Nutritional Info: 332 Cal; 17 g Fats; 34 g Protein; 7 g Net Carb; 1 g Fiber;

Ingredients

- 1 ¼ pound shrimp, tail removed, peeled, de-veined
- 1 ½ tablespoon minced garlic
- 2 scallions, sliced
- ¾ teaspoon salt
- ½ teaspoon ground black pepper
- ¼ teaspoon red pepper flakes
- ¼ cup chopped parsley
- 4 tablespoons butter, unsalted
- ¼ cup lemon juice
- ¼ cup chardonnay
- ½ cup shredded Parmesan cheese

Directions

- Take a large skillet pan, place it over medium heat, add butter and when it melts, add garlic and cook for 1 minute until tender and golden brown.
- Add shrimps, cook them for 3 to 4 minutes until bottom turns pink, then flip the shrimps by using tongs, sprinkle with red pepper flakes, and continue cooking for 3 minutes.
- Then drizzle wine and lemon juice over shrimps, cook another minute and then remove the pan from heat.
- Sprinkle scallions and parsley over the shrimps, season with salt and black pepper, and then top with cheese.
- Serve straight away.

Lobster Cheddar Bay Biscuits

Serving: 9
Preparation time: 10 minutes; Cooking time: 11 minutes;
Nutritional Info: 240 Cal; 22 g Fats; 7 g Protein; 3 g Net Carb; 0.5 g Fiber;
Ingredients
- 1 ½ cups almond flour
- 1 teaspoon garlic powder
- ¼ teaspoon salt
- 1 tablespoon baking powder
- ½ cup shredded cheddar cheese
- ½ cup sour cream
- 4 tablespoons butter, unsalted, melted
- 2 eggs

For the Topping:
- ½ teaspoon garlic powder
- 2 tablespoons butter, unsalted, melted
- 1 tablespoon minced parsley

Directions
- Switch on the oven, then set it to 450 degrees F and let it preheat.
- Take a large bowl, place flour in it and then stir in garlic, baking powder, and salt until combined.
- Take a small bowl, crack the eggs in it, whisk in butter and sour cream until smooth, and then stir in almond flour mixture until smooth batter comes together.
- Take a 12-cups muffin pan, grease the cups with oi, evenly fill them with batter and then bake for 11 minutes until the top of each biscuit turns golden brown and inserted toothpick into each biscuit comes out clean.
- Meanwhile, take a small bowl, place melted butter in it, stir in garlic powder until dissolved and then stir in parsley.
- When done, remove biscuit from the pan, transfer them to a baking sheet and then immediately brush the garlic-parsley butter on top of each biscuit.
- Serve straight away.

Fish and Chips

Serving: 2

Preparation time: 15 minutes; Cooking time: 30 minutes;

Nutritional Info: 884 Cal; 70 g Fats; 51 g Protein; 10 g Net Carb; 5 g Fiber;

Ingredients

For the Chips:
- 1 medium zucchini
- ¼ teaspoon salt
- ¼ teaspoon ground black pepper
- ½ tablespoon avocado oil

For the fish:
- ¾ pound cod
- ½ cup almond flour
- ¼ teaspoon onion Powder
- ½ teaspoon salt
- 1/3 teaspoon ground black pepper
- ½ teaspoon paprika powder
- 4 cups avocado oil
- 1 egg
- ½ cup grated Parmesan cheese

For the Dipping Sauce:
- ¼ tablespoon curry powder
- 2 tablespoons dill pickle relish
- ½ cup mayonnaise

Directions
- Prepare the dipping sauce and for this, take a medium bowl, place all of its ingredients in it, whisk until combined, and then set aside until required.
- Switch on the oven, then set it to 400 degrees F and let it preheat.
- Meanwhile, cut the zucchini into thin fries, place them in a medium bowl, drizzle with oil and then toss until coated.

- Spread the zucchini pieces on a baking sheet, season with salt and black pepper, and then bake for 30 minutes until golden brown, tossing halfway.
- Meanwhile, prepare the fish and for this, crack the egg in a shallow dish and then whisk until frothy.
- Take a separate shallow dish, place flour in it, add all the spices and cheese, and then stir until combined.
- Cut the dish into a 1-by-1 inch piece, dredge each piece into the almond flour mixture, dip into egg, and then dredge again with almond flour mixture.
- Take a large skillet pan, place it over medium heat, add oil, let it heat for 12 minutes until it reaches to 360 degrees F, then add prepared fish pieces and cook them for 4 minutes per side until golden brown and cooked.
- Divide baked zucchini fries evenly between two plates, add fried fish and then serve with the dipping sauce.

LUNCH – PORK RECIPES

Pulled Pork

Serving: 8
Preparation time: 10 minutes; Cooking time: 8 hours;
Nutritional Info: 511 Cal; 37 g Fats; 40 g Protein; 2 g Net Carb; 0 g Fiber;
Ingredients
- 3 pounds pork shoulder, boneless, excess fat trimmed
- 2 teaspoons onion powder
- 2 teaspoons garlic powder
- 2 teaspoons salt
- 1 tablespoon dried parsley
- 2 teaspoons cumin
- 2 teaspoons paprika
- ½ cup beer
- 8 lettuce leaves
Directions
- Switch on a 1-quarts slow cooker and then place pork in it.
- Take a small bowl, add all the spices in it, stir until mixed, and then rub this mixture on all sides of the pork until well coated.
- Pour in the beer, shut with the lid, and then cook for 8 hours at low heat setting or for 4 hours at high heat setting until fork tender.
- When done, shred the pork by using two forks, and then stir until well mixed with its juices.
- Top pork over lettuce leaves and then serve.

Texas-Style Pork Belly

Serving: 12

Preparation time: 10 minutes; Cooking time: 8 hours;

Nutritional Info: 979 Cal; 100.1 g Fats; 19.6 g Protein; 0 g Net Carb; 0 g Fiber;

Ingredients

- 5 pounds pork belly, boneless, skinless
- 3 tablespoons salt
- ¼ cup ground black pepper

Directions

- Take a small bowl, add salt in it, stir in black pepper and then rub this mixture on all sides of the pork belly until well coated.
- Prepare the grill, let it preheat at medium-high heat setting, and when ready to grill, place the pork belly on it and then grill for 6 to 8 hours until the internal temperature of the pork reaches to 195 degrees F.
- When done, wrap the pork belly with foil and let it rest for a minimum of 1 hour.
- Then cut the pork belly into slices and serve.

Parmesan Pork Chops

Serving: 2
Preparation time: 5 minutes; Cooking time: 10 minutes;
Nutritional Info: 370 Cal; 26 g Fats; 32 g Protein; 1 g Net Carb; 0 g Fiber;
Ingredients
- 4 pork chops, boneless
- ½ teaspoon garlic powder
- ¼ teaspoon salt
- ¼ teaspoon ground white pepper
- 2 tablespoons avocado oil
- 1 egg
- 4 ounces shredded parmesan cheese

Directions
- Take a small bowl, place garlic powder in it, add salt and black pepper, and then stir until mixed.
- Sprinkle the spice mixture on both sides of the pork chops and then press into it.
- Take a shallow dish, crack the egg in it and then beat until frothy.
- Take a separate shallow dish, place parmesan cheese on it.
- Dip each pork chop into the egg and then coat with cheese.
- Take a frying pan, place it over medium-high heat, add oil and when hot, add a prepared pork chop in it and then cook for 5 minutes per side until browned and tender.
- When done, transfer pork chops to a plate and then repeat with the remaining chops.
- Serve straight away with cauliflower mash.

DINNER – BEEF RECIPES

Chipotle Beef Barbacoa

Serving: 9
Preparation time: 10 minutes; Cooking time: 10 hours;
Nutritional Info: 242 Cal; 11 g Fats; 32 g Protein; 1 g Net Carb; 1 g Fiber;
Ingredients
- 3 pounds beef brisket, fat trimmed, 2-inch cubed
- 2 medium chipotle chilies in adobo sauce
- 2 ½ tablespoons minced garlic
- 2 teaspoons sea salt
- 1 teaspoon ground black pepper
- 1 tablespoon dried oregano
- 2 teaspoons cumin
- ½ teaspoon ground cloves
- 2 bay leaves
- 2 tablespoons lime juice
- 2 tablespoons apple cider vinegar
- 4 teaspoons adobo sauce
- ½ cup beef broth

Directions
- Plug in a food processor, add all the ingredients in it except for beef pieces and bay leaves and then pulse for 2 minutes until smooth.
- Plug in a 4-quarts slow cooker, place beef pieces in it, top with blended mixture, add bay leaves, and then cover with the lid.
- Cook the beef for 6 hours at a high heat setting or for 10 hours at a low heat setting until tender.
- When done, uncover the slow cooker, remove the bay leaves and then shred the beef by using two forks.
- Stir the beef into its juices, cover the slow cooker with its lid and then let it rest for 10 minutes.
- Serve straight away with cauliflower rice.

PF Chang's Beef and Broccoli

Serving: 4

Preparation time: 10 minutes; Cooking time: 10 minutes;

Nutritional Info: 271 Cal; 12 g Fats; 35.2 g Protein; 3.5 g Net Carb; 2 g Fiber;

Ingredients

- 1 pound steak, cut into ¼-inch thick slices
- 1 large head broccoli, cut into small florets
- 2 scallions, chopped
- 1 tablespoon minced garlic
- 2 slices of ginger, peeled, chopped
- 2 teaspoons sesame seeds
- 2 tablespoons avocado oil
- 2 tablespoons water

For the Marinade:

- 1 ½ teaspoon minced garlic
- 1 teaspoon grated ginger
- ¼ teaspoon baking soda
- ½ teaspoon of sea salt
- ¼ teaspoon crushed red pepper
- 2 tablespoons coconut aminos
- 1 tablespoon sesame oil

For the Sauce:

- 1 tablespoon red boat fish sauce, low-carb
- 2 tablespoons coconut aminos
- 2 teaspoons sesame oil
- ½ teaspoon ground black pepper

Directions

- Prepare the sauce and for this, take a small bowl, place all of its ingredients in it and then stir until well combined, set aside until required.

- Prepare the marinade and for this, take a small bowl, place all of its ingredients in it and then stir until well combined.
- Add beef pieces into the marinade and let it rest in the refrigerator for a minimum of 15 minutes.
- Meanwhile, place broccoli florets into a large heatproof bowl, drizzle with water, cover with a plastic wrap, and then microwave for 3 minutes until florets turn tender-crisp, set aside until required.
- Take a large skillet pan, place it over medium-high heat, add 1 tablespoon of oil and when hot, add garlic and ginger, stir in salt and cook for 15 seconds until fragrant.
- Switch heat to the high level, add marinated beef pieces, and then cook for 2 minutes per side until its edges turn golden brown.
- Pour in the sauce, toss until combined, cook for 1 minute, then add broccoli florets and cook for 30 seconds.
- Garnish broccoli and beef with sesame seeds and then serve.

Big Mac Salad

Serving: 4

Preparation time: 5 minutes; Cooking time: 20 minutes;

Nutritional Info: 273 Cal; 21 g Fats; 19 g Protein; 2 g Net Carb; 1 g Fiber;

Ingredients

For the Salad:

- 12 ounces of lettuce greens
- ½ of small white onion, peeled, chopped
- 1 small red onion, peeled sliced
- 3 small tomatoes, sliced
- 2 spears of dill pickles, diced
- 1 1/3 pounds ground beef
- 2 tablespoons minced garlic
- 1 teaspoon salt
- ½ teaspoon ground black pepper
- 1/8 teaspoon red chili pepper
- 1/8 teaspoon dried thyme
- ¼ teaspoon marjoram
- ¼ teaspoon ground oregano
- 2 tablespoons avocado oil
- ¾ cup grated cheddar cheese

For the Dressing:

- ¼ teaspoon salt
- 1/8 teaspoon dried basil
- ¼ teaspoon ground black pepper
- 1/8 teaspoon cayenne pepper
- 2 tablespoons tomato paste
- 1/8 teaspoon ground sage
- ¼ cup sour cream
- 1/8 teaspoon ground oregano

- 3 tablespoons water
- 1/3 cup mayonnaise

Directions

- Prepare the dressing and for this, take a medium bowl, place all of its ingredients in it and whisk until smooth, set aside until required.
- Take a large skillet pan, place it over medium heat, add oil and when hot, add white onion and cook for 5 minutes until translucent.
- Add garlic, cook for 1 minute until fragrant, then add ground beef, add all the seasonings and spices and cook for 10 to 12 minutes until beef has thoroughly cooked.
- Assemble the bowl and for this, take a large platter, cover it with beef, layer it with tomato, lettuce, green onion, and pickle and then sprinkle with cheese.
- Drizzle the prepared dressing over the top and then serve.

Outback Steakhouse Charcoal Ribeye

Serving: 4

Preparation time: 10 minutes; Cooking time: 10 minutes;

Nutritional Info: 629 Cal; 41 g Fats; 58 g Protein; 8 g Net Carb; 1 g Fiber;

Ingredients

- 4 ribeye steaks, fat trimmed, cut into 1 ½-inch thick slices
- 2 teaspoons salt
- 2 teaspoons ground black pepper

For the Seasoning:

- 2 tablespoon erythritol sweetener
- 1 teaspoon turmeric powder
- 2 teaspoon smoked paprika
- 1 teaspoon red chili powder
- 4 tablespoons steak seasoning

Directions

- Prepare the steak and for this, bring it to room temperature and then season well with salt and black pepper.
- Prepare the grill by lighting the charcoals, place the cooking grate in it, cover the grill with its lid, and let it preheat for 5 minutes.
- Brush the grate with oil generously, then place a prepared steak onto hottest the cooking grate and sear it for 3 minutes.
- Then flip the steak, continue grilling for 3 minutes, transfer it to the warmer side of the cooking grate, and repeat with the remaining steaks.
- Then shut the grill with its lid and continue cooking the steak until it has cooked to the desired doneness.
- When done, remove steaks from the grill, cover them with foil and let them rest for 5 minutes.
- Cut the steak into slices across the grain and then serve.

DINNER – POULTRY RECIPES

Tso's Chicken

Serving: 4
Preparation time: 10 minutes; Cooking time: 20 minutes;
Nutritional Info: 427 Cal; 30 g Fats; 35 g Protein; 1 g Net Carb; 2 g Fiber;
Ingredients
For the Chicken:
- 1 ½ pounds chicken thighs, boneless
- 1 green onion, chopped
- ½ cup almond flour
- ¼ teaspoon salt
- ¼ teaspoon ground black pepper
- ½ teaspoon xanthan gum
- 2 egg whites
- 2 tablespoons coconut oil
- ½ cup chicken broth
- 1 teaspoon sesame seeds

For the Sauce:
- 1 ½ tablespoon minced garlic
- ½ teaspoon grated ginger
- 1 teaspoon Swerve sweetener
- 1 teaspoon red chili paste
- 5 tablespoons soy sauce
- 2 tablespoons ketchup, sugar-free
- 1 teaspoon sesame oil

Directions
- Prepare the sauce and for this, take a medium bowl, place all of its ingredients in it and then whisk until combined, set aside until required.

- Prepare the chicken and for this, cut it into bite-size pieces and then season it with salt and black pepper.
- Take a shallow dish, crack the egg in it and whisk until frothy.
- Take a separate shallow dish and then spread flour in it.
- Working on one chicken piece at a time, first dip it into the egg, dredge it into the flour until coated, and repeat with the remaining pieces.
- Plugin the instant pot, press the 'sauté' button, add oil and when hot, add chicken pieces in a single layer and then cook them for 3 to 4 minutes per side until golden brown.
- Transfer the chicken pieces to a plate and repeat with the remaining chicken pieces.
- When done, stir broth into the inner pot to remove browned bits from the bottom of the pot, return chicken pieces into the pot and pour the prepared sauce over them.
- Shut the instant pot with its lid in the sealed position, press the manual button, and let the chicken cook for 4 minutes.
- When the instant pot, do a quick pressure release, then open the instant pot and stir xanthan gum into the chicken until sauce thickens.
- Top chicken with sesame seeds and green onions and serve with cauliflower rice.

Applebee's Fiesta Lime Chicken

Serving: 4
Preparation time: 10 minutes; Cooking time: 13 minutes;
Nutritional Info: 294 Cal; 14.5 g Fats; 33.2 g Protein; 6.1 g Net Carb; 0.3 g Fiber;
Ingredients

- 1 pound chicken breast
- 1 cup shredded Colby-Monterey jack cheese

For the Marinade:

- 1 ½ teaspoon minced garlic
- ¼ teaspoon ginger powder
- ½ teaspoon salt
- 1 teaspoon liquid smoke
- ½ of lime, juiced
- 1/3 cup teriyaki sauce
- 1 teaspoon tequila
- 1 cup of water

For the Dressing:

- 1 teaspoon Cajun spice mix
- ¼ teaspoon dried parsley
- 1/8 teaspoon cumin
- 1/8 teaspoon dried dill
- ¼ teaspoon hot sauce
- 2 tablespoons spicy salsa, low-carb
- 1 tablespoon coconut milk, unsweetened
- ¼ cup sour cream
- ¼ cup mayonnaise

Directions

- Prepare the marinade and for this, take a large bowl, place all of its ingredients in it and then whisk until combined.

- Add chicken, toss until well coated and then let the chicken marinate in the refrigerator for a minimum of 2 hours.
- Meanwhile, prepare the dressing and for this, take a large bowl, place all of its ingredients in it, whisk until combined, and let it rest in the refrigerator until chilled.
- When the chicken has marinated, set up the grill and let it preheat at a high heat setting for 5 minutes.
- Place chicken on the cooking grate and then cook it for 5 minutes per side until thoroughly cooked.
- When done, brush the chicken generously with prepared dressing, arrange chicken in a baking sheet, sprinkle cheese on top, and then broil for 3 minutes until cheese has melted.
- Serve chicken straight away.

Garcia's Pollo Fundido

Serving: 4

Preparation time: 10 minutes; Cooking time: 45 minutes;

Nutritional Info: 520 Cal; 25 g Fats; 62 g Protein; 5 g Net Carb; 0 g Fiber;

Ingredients

- 2 pounds of chicken breasts
- 4 ounces diced green chilies
- ½ teaspoon garlic powder
- ¼ teaspoon of sea salt
- ¼ teaspoon ground black pepper
- ¼ teaspoon cumin
- 8 ounces cream cheese, softened
- 1 cup Monterrey jack cheese

Directions

- Switch on the oven, then set it to 375 degrees F and let it preheat.
- Meanwhile, take a large bowl, place cream cheese in it, add all the seasoning and spices, stir well until well combined, and then fold in the green chilies until incorporated.
- Take a large baking dish, place chicken breasts in it with some space between them, and spread cream cheese mixture on the top evenly.
- Sprinkle cheese on the top and then bake for 45 minutes until the chicken has thoroughly cooked.
- When done, let the chicken cool for 5 minutes and then serve.

Popeye's Chicken Strips

Serving: 6

Preparation time: 10 minutes; Cooking time: 20 minutes;

Nutritional Info: 385 Cal; 25 g Fats; 35 g Protein; 4 g Net Carb; 1 g Fiber;

Ingredients

- 2 pounds of chicken breasts
- 2/3 cup almond flour
- 2 teaspoons salt
- 1 teaspoon chipotle chili powder
- 2 teaspoons smoked paprika
- 1/3 cup Louisiana style hot sauce, low-carb
- 3 eggs
- ½ cup almond milk, unsweetened
- Avocado oil as needed for frying

Directions

- Take a small bowl, pour in the milk, and then whisk in hot sauce.
- Cut each chicken breast into four strips, place them into a large bowl, pour in half of the milk mixture, and then marinate for a minimum of 1 hour.
- Then take a shallow dish, place flour in it, and stir in salt, paprika, and chipotle until mixed.
- Crack the eggs into the remaining milk mixture and then whisk until frothy.
- When the chicken has marinated, drain it well, dredge each chicken strip into the flour mixture, dip into the egg mixture and dredge again in flour mixture.
- When ready to cook, take a large skillet pan, fill it 2 ½-inches of oil, place the pan over medium-high heat and bring the oil to 360 degrees F.
- Then lower the chicken pieces into the oil, don't overcrowd it, and then cook for 5 to 7 minutes per side until cooked and golden brown.
- Transfer chicken pieces to a plate lined with paper towels and then repeat with the remaining chicken pieces.
- Serve straight away.

Olive Garden's Chicken Piccata

Serving: 5

Preparation time: 10 minutes; Cooking time: 15 minutes;

Nutritional Info: 309 Cal; 15 g Fats; 43 g Protein; 0.3 g Net Carb; 0.3 g Fiber;

Ingredients

- 2 pounds chicken breasts, thinly sliced
- 2 tablespoons chopped parsley
- ¼ cup drained capers, rinsed
- ½ teaspoon salt
- ½ teaspoon ground black pepper
- 1/3 cup lemon juice
- 2 tablespoons avocado oil
- 4 tablespoons butter, unsalted, divided
- ½ cup chicken broth

Directions

- Prepare the chicken and for this, pound the chicken with a meat mallet and then season with salt and black pepper.
- Take a large skillet pan, place it over medium-high heat, add oil and 2 tablespoons of butter and when hot, add chicken until the pan is filled and then cook for 2 minutes per side until nicely golden brown.
- When done, transfer chicken to a plate and then repeat with the remaining chicken.
- When done, stir lemon juice and broth into the pan to remove browned bits from the pan, add capers and then bring the mixture to a boil.
- Return chicken into the pan, simmer for 2 minutes, and then transfer chicken pieces to a plate.
- Add remaining butter into the pan, whisk it until combined, and then drizzle the sauce over chicken.
- Garnish the chicken with parsley and then serve.

California Pizza's Cobb Salad with Ranch Dressing

Serving: 2

Preparation time: 10 minutes; Cooking time: 0 minutes;

Nutritional Info: 945 Cal; 81 g Fats; 43 g Protein; 6 g Net Carb; 9 g Fiber;

Ingredients

For the Ranch dressing

- 1 tablespoon ranch seasoning
- 3 tablespoons mayonnaise
- 2 tablespoons water

For the Salad:

- ½ pound rotisserie chicken
- 3 ounces bacon, cooked
- 5 ounces Romaine lettuce, chopped
- 1 medium tomato, sliced
- 1 medium avocado, pitted, peeled, sliced
- 1 tablespoon minced chives
- ½ teaspoon salt
- 1/3 teaspoon ground black pepper
- 2 eggs, boiled
- 2 ounces blue cheese, crumbled

Directions

- Prepare the dressing and for this, take a small bowl, place all of its ingredients in it and then whisk until combined.
- Assemble the salad and for this, cut the chicken into small pieces and then distribute evenly between two bowls.
- Peeled the boiled eggs, cut into slices, and evenly distribute into the salad bowls.
- Add vegetables, cheese and bacon, season the salad with salt and black pepper and then drizzle the prepared dressing on top.
- Sprinkle chives on top and then serve.

DINNER – FISH AND SEAFOOD RECIPES

The Cheesecake Factory's Tuna Tataki Salad

Serving: 4
Preparation time: 10 minutes; Cooking time: 5 minutes;
Nutritional Info: 594 Cal; 42.2 g Fats; 37.1 g Protein; 4.4 g Net Carb; 12 g Fiber;
Ingredients
For the Tuna:

- 1 pound tuna, sashimi grade
- 4 tablespoons avocado oil

For the Salad:

- 4 radishes, peeled, sliced thinly
- 8 cups salad greens
- 4 green onion, sliced
- 4 avocados, peeled, pitted, sliced
- 2 teaspoons black sesame seeds

For the Salad Dressing:

- 2 1-inch pieces of ginger, grated
- 2 tablespoons liquid stevia
- 4 tablespoons ponzu sauce, low-carb
- 2 tablespoons sake
- 2 tablespoons soy sauce
- 2 tablespoons toasted sesame oil

Directions

- Prepare the salad dressing and for this, take a mason jar, place all of its ingredients in it, shut with the lid, and then shake well until well blended, set aside until required.
- Take a large salad bowl, place avocado slices, radish, and salad greens in it, and then toss until mixed.

- Prepare the tuna and for this, take a large skillet pan, place it over medium heat, add oil and when hot, add tuna and then cook for 1 minute per side until seared.
- Transfer tuna to a plate, repeat with the remaining tuna, let cool for 15 minutes and then cut tuna into thin slices.
- Distribute salad evenly among four plates, add seared tuna to the side and then drizzle with prepared salad dressing.
- Sprinkle sesame seeds and green onion over tuna and then serve.

Outback Steakhouse's Coconut Shrimp

Serving: 4

Preparation time: 10 minutes; Cooking time: 14 minutes;

Nutritional Info: 335 Cal; 15.6 g Fats; 46.1 g Protein; 0.9 g Net Carb; 1.7 g Fiber;

Ingredients

- 1 pound medium shrimp, tail removed, peeled, deveined, cooked
- ½ cup pork rind
- 1 teaspoon salt
- ½ cup shredded coconut, unsweetened
- ½ teaspoon ground black pepper
- ¼ cup coconut milk, unsweetened

Directions

- Take a shallow pan, place it over low heat and when hot, add coconut and cook for 3 to 4 minutes until golden brown.
- Take a shallow dish, and then pour in the milk.
- Take a separate shallow dish, place coconut and pork rind in it, and then stir until mixed.
- Pat dry the shrimp with paper towels, then dip each shrimp into milk and dredge in the pork-coconut mixture until evenly coated.
- Plugin the air fryer, insert a greased fryer basket, set it 400 degrees F, and let it preheat for 400 degrees F.
- Then add shrimps in a single layer into the fryer basket and then fry for 7 minutes, shaking halfway.
- When done, transfer fried shrimps to a plate and repeat with the remaining shrimps.
- Season the shrimps with salt and black pepper and then serve.

Bang Bang Shrimp

Serving: 4

Preparation time: 10 minutes; Cooking time: 12 minutes;

Nutritional Info: 204 Cal; 16 g Fats; 20 g Protein; 3 g Net Carb; 3 g Fiber;

Ingredients

For the Shrimp:

- 1 pound shrimp, tail removed, peeled, deveined
- ½ cup coconut flour
- Avocado oil as needed for frying
- 1 scallion, sliced

For the Sauce:

- 1/3 cup mayonnaise
- 1 ¾ tablespoon garlic chili sauce
- 1 ½ tablespoon rice vinegar
- 2 ½ tablespoons monk fruit Sweetener
- 1/8 teaspoon salt

Directions

- Prepare the shrimps and for this, dredge each shrimp in coconut flour and then arrange on a baking sheet.
- Then take a large skillet pan, place it over medium-high heat, fill it 2-inch with oil and when hot, add shrimps in it and then cook for 4 minutes or more until pink.
- When done, transfer shrimps to a plate lined with paper towels and repeat with the remaining shrimps.
- Prepare the sauce and for this, plug in a food processor, add all the ingredients in it, cover with the lid, and then pulse for 30 seconds until smooth.
- Tip the sauce into a large bowl, add shrimps and then toss until coated.
- Garnish shrimps with scallion and then serve.

Fish Cakes

Serving: 2

Preparation time: 5 minutes; Cooking time: 16 minutes;

Nutritional Info: 69 Cal; 6.5 g Fats; 1.1 g Protein; 0.6 g Net Carb; 1.1 g Fiber;

Ingredients

For the Fish Cake:

- 1 pound white fish, boneless
- ¼ cup cilantro leaves
- ¼ teaspoon salt
- ¼ teaspoon red chili flakes
- 1 tablespoon minced garlic
- 2 tablespoons avocado oil

For the Dip:

- 1 lemon, juiced
- 2 avocados, peeled, pitted
- ¼ teaspoon salt
- 2 tablespoons water

Directions

- Prepare the fish cakes and for this, place all of its ingredients in a food processor except for oil and then pulse for 3 minutes until well combined.
- Tip the mixture in a large bowl and then shape it into six patties.
- Take a frying pan, place it over medium-high heat, add oil and when hot, add fish patties in it and then cook for 3 to 4 minutes per side until cooked and golden brown.
- Meanwhile, prepare the dip and for this, place all of its ingredients in a food processor and then pulse for 2 minutes until smooth.
- Serve fish cakes with prepared dip.

DINNER – PORK RECIPES

Chili's BBQ Baby Back Ribs

Serving: 6
Preparation time: 10 minutes; Cooking time: 3 hours;
Nutritional Info: 445 Cal; 32.5 g Fats; 37 g Protein; 2.7 g Net Carb; 0.6 g Fiber;
Ingredients
- 2 full racks of baby back ribs, membrane removed
- 2 teaspoons salt
- 1 ½ teaspoon ground black pepper
- 2 tablespoons dry barbecue rub
- 2 tablespoons avocado oil, divided
- 1/2 cup BBQ Sauce, low-carb

Directions
- Switch on the oven, set the baking rack in the middle of it, then set it to 275 degrees F and let it preheat.
- Meanwhile, prepare the ribs and for this, brush each side of ribs with ½ tablespoon oil and then massage ½ tablespoon of barbecue rub on each side.
- Place the seasoned ribs onto a rimmed baking sheet, seal the rib along with the pan with foil and then bake for 2 hours and 30 minutes until fork tender.
- Then uncover the ribs, season with some more salt, black pepper, and barbecue rub and continue baking for 30 minutes.
- When done, let ribs rest for 10 minutes, then cut into slices and serve.

Antipasto Salad

Serving: 4

Preparation time: 10 minutes; Cooking time: 0 minutes;

Nutritional Info: 824 Cal; 65 g Fats; 38 g Protein; 13 g Net Carb; 9 g Fiber;

Ingredients

- 20 ounces Romaine lettuce
- 6 ounces prosciutto, thinly sliced
- 2 ounces drained sun-dried tomatoes, chopped
- 6 ounces salami, thinly sliced
- 2 ounces whole olives, pitted
- 10 ounces drained artichokes, quartered
- 2 red chili peppers, chopped
- 6 ounces roasted red peppers
- 4 tablespoons chopped parsley,
- 2/3 cup basil, fresh
- 1 tablespoon of sea salt
- 10 ounces mozzarella cheese, sliced in small pieces
- 8 tablespoons avocado oil

Directions

- Take a small bowl, place basil in it, add salt and chili pepper, and then crush by using a wooden spoon.
- Chop the lettuce, then distribute evenly among four salad plates and add parsley.
- Layer the lettuce with the remaining ingredients except for oil and then sprinkle red pepper mixture on top.
- Drizzle the salad with oil and then serve.

Garlic and Parmesan Pork Chops

Serving: 6

Preparation time: 10 minutes; Cooking time: 20 minutes;

Nutritional Info: 438 Cal; 33 g Fats; 30 g Protein; 2.5 g Net Carb; 0.2 g Fiber;

Ingredients

- ½ of a medium white onion, peeled, sliced
- 1 ½ pound center-cut pork chops, boneless
- 1 tablespoon minced garlic
- 1 teaspoon salt
- ½ teaspoon ground black pepper
- 1 tablespoon Italian seasoning
- 2 tablespoons avocado oil
- ½ cup grated cheddar cheese
- 1-ounce cream cheese, softened
- 1/3 cup parmesan cheese
- 1 cup heavy whipping cream
- 1/3 cup chicken broth

Directions

- Take a large skillet pan, place it over medium-high heat, add oil and when hot, add pork chops and cook for 5 minutes per side until nicely browned.
- Transfer the pork chops to a plate, add onion and garlic to the pan and then cook for 5 minutes until tender.
- Add remaining ingredients, stir until mixed, switch heat to the medium sauce, and then cook for 3 to 5 minutes until the sauce has thickened.
- Return pork chops into the pan, toss until coated with the sauce, then switch heat to the low level and simmer for 5 minutes until done.
- Serve straight away.

SNACKS AND APPETIZERS

Bloomin' Onion

Serving: 4

Preparation time: 15 minutes; Cooking time: 5 minutes;

Nutritional Info: 524 Cal; 30.3 g Fats; 47.2 g Protein; 10 g Net Carb; 5.8 g Fiber;

Ingredients

- 1 large sweet onion
- ½ cup coconut flour
- ½ tablespoon seasoning salt
- ½ teaspoon ground black pepper
- ½ teaspoon cayenne
- ½ tablespoon paprika
- 4 tablespoons heavy whipping cream
- 4 eggs
- 1 cup pork rind
- Avocado oil, as needed for frying

Directions

- Prepare the onion and for this, remove ¼ top off the onion, flip it cut-side-down and then cut it into quarters in such a way that there is only ¼-inch space from the onion nub.
- Cut the quarters into eights and then cut them into sixteenths.
- Sprinkle coconut flour generously over the onion until each petal and the bottom of onion have coated.
- Prepare the egg wash and for this, take a medium bowl, crack the eggs in it, whisk in the cream until blended, and then spoon half of this mixture over the onion until each petal, and the bottom of onion have coated.
- Take a separate medium bowl, place pork rind in it, add all the seasonings, stir until mixed, and then coat onion inside out with this mixture.

- Repeat by pouring the remaining egg wash over the onion and dredge again into pork rind mixture.
- Transfer onion onto a plate and then freeze it for 1 hour.
- When ready to cook, take a large pot, place it over medium-high heat, fill it two-third with oil, and bring it to 300 degrees F temperature.
- Then lower the frozen onion into the oil, petal-side-down, cook for 1 month, switch heat to medium-low level, flip the onion and fry it for 3 minutes.
- Transfer onion to a plate lined with paper towels and let it rest for 5 minutes.
- Serve the onion with dipping sauce.

Brined Chicken Bites

Serving: 4
Preparation time: 10 minutes; Cooking time: 20 minutes;
Nutritional Info: 284 Cal; 17 g Fats; 34 g Protein; 1 g Net Carb; 0 g Fiber;
Ingredients
- 1 pound chicken breast
- ½ teaspoon salt
- 2 cups pickle juice
- Avocado oil, as needed for frying

For the Coating:
- 1 tablespoon baking powder
- ½ teaspoon garlic powder
- ½ teaspoon salt
- 1 tablespoon erythritol sweetener
- ½ teaspoon ground black pepper
- ½ teaspoon paprika
- ½ cup whey protein powder

Directions
- Cut the chicken into 1-inch pieces, place them in a large plastic bag, add salt, pour in pickle juice, and then seal the bag.
- Turn it upside down to coat the chicken pieces and then let marinate for a minimum of 30 minutes in the refrigerator.
- Then remove chicken from the refrigerator, let it rest at room temperature for 25 minutes, drain it well, and pat dry with paper towels.
- Cook the chicken and for this, take a large pot, place it over medium-low heat, pour in oil until the pot has half-full, and then bring it to 350 degrees F.
- Meanwhile, prepare the coating and for this, take a medium bowl, place all of its ingredients in it and then stir until mixed.
- Dredge a chicken piece into the coating mixture until thoroughly covered, arrange it onto a baking sheet lined with parchment paper and repeat with the remaining pieces.
- Drop the prepared chicken pieces into the oil, fry for 6 minutes until thoroughly cooked, and then transfer to a plate lined with paper towels.
- Repeat with the remaining chicken pieces and then serve.

Pepperoni Chips

Serving: 2

Preparation time: 5 minutes; Cooking time: 8 minutes;

Nutritional Info: 150 Cal; 14 g Fats; 5 g Protein; 1 g Net Carb; 0 g Fiber;

Ingredients

- 30 pepperoni slices

Directions

- Switch on the oven, set it to 400 degrees F, then set the baking rack in the middle and let it preheat.
- Meanwhile, take a sheet pan or two, line with parchment paper and then spread pepperoni slices o with some spacing between each slice.
- Bake the pepperoni slices for 4 minutes, then pat dry them with paper towels and then continue baking them for 4 minutes until nicely golden brown.
- When done, drain the pepperoni slices on paper towels and then serve.

Crispy Cheesy Chips

Serving: 8
Preparation time: 10 minutes; Cooking time: 10 minutes;
Nutritional Info: 164 Cal; 0.4 g Fats; 36.8 g Protein; 0.8 g Net Carb; 0.9 g Fiber;
Ingredients
- 1 cup whey protein isolate
- 4 cups shredded mozzarella cheese
Directions
- Take a medium heatproof bowl, place cheese in it, and then microwave for 1 minute until cheese melts.
- Remove bowl from the oven and immediately stir in whey protein until well combined and the dough comes together.
- Spread a sheet of parchment on working space, place half of the dough on it, and then cover it with the parchment sheet of the same size.
- Shape the dough into a thin rectangle by using hands and rolling pin and then cut out triangles by using a pizza cutter.
- Repeat with the remaining dough to make more chips.
- Transfer the cheese triangles onto two large baking sheets, leaving some space between them and then bake for 8 to 10 minutes until nicely browned.
- When done, let the chips cool for 5 minutes and then serve with a dip.

PASTA

Carbonara Pasta

Serving: 2

Preparation time: 10 minutes; Cooking time: 25 minutes;

Nutritional Info: 580 Cal; 50 g Fats; 27 g Protein; 4 g Net Carb; 1 g Fiber;

Ingredients

- 4 ounces chicken breast, diced
- 10-ounce bacon, diced
- 2 cups heavy whipping
- 4 tablespoons grated parmesan cheese
- 2 egg yolk
- 2 packets of miracle noodles, cooked

Directions

- Take a large skillet pan, place it over medium heat, add bacon and cook for 7 to 10 minutes until nicely golden brown.
- Transfer bacon to a bowl, add chicken to the pan, cook for 10 minutes or more until golden brown and then transfer it to the bowl containing bacon.
- Take a small bowl, place egg yolks in it, add cheese, and then stir well until the smooth paste comes together.
- While the chicken cooked, prepare the noodles, and for this, fry them in a separate pan for 10 minutes or more according to the instructions on the packet, set aside until required.
- Return the skillet pan over medium heat, pour 1 cup cream, add parmesan-egg mixture and whisk well until smooth.
- Add remaining cream into the pan, return bacon and chicken in it, toss until well mixed and cook them for 2 minutes or more until hot.
- Add noodles into the pan, toss until well coated with the sauce, and then serve.

Singapore Noodles with Chicken, Shrimp, and Bacon

Serving: 2
Preparation time: 10 minutes; Cooking time: 15 minutes;
Nutritional Info: 417 Cal; 29 g Fats; 23 g Protein; 6 g Net Carb; 6 g Fiber;
Ingredients
- 10 ounces chicken thigh, boneless, thinly sliced
- 6 ounces shrimp, peeled, deveined, cooked, chopped
- 4 slices of bacon
- 4 ounces bean sprouts
- 2 small white onions, peeled, sliced
- 2 bunches of bok choy, sliced
- 1 tablespoon minced garlic
- 2 stick of celery, sliced
- 4 teaspoons curry powder
- 4 tablespoons coconut aminos
- 2 tablespoons sesame oil
- 16 ounces shirataki noodles

Directions
- Prepare the noodles and for this, place noodles into a large bowl, pour in hot water, let them soak for 6 minutes, then drain them well and set aside until required.
- Then take a large frying pan, place it over high heat, add oil and when hot, add bacon and cook for 1 minute or until sauté.
- Add chicken pieces, cook for 3 minutes until nicely golden brown on all sides, then add onion and garlic and continue cooking for 2 minutes until vegetables begin to tender.
- Add shrimps and celery, season with curry powder, stir well until combined, and then push all the ingredients to the side of the pan to create a well in its center.
- Add noodles into the center of the pan, stir with all the ingredients until combined, cook for 2 minutes and then drizzle with coconut aminos.
- Add sprouts and bok choy, toss until all the ingredients are coated with coconut aminos and well combined, and then cook for 2 minutes until the vegetables have turned slightly soft.
- Serve straight away.

Zucchini Noodle Alfredo

Serving: 8

Preparation time: 10 minutes; Cooking time: 20 minutes;

Nutritional Info: 743 Cal; 73.2 g Fats; 15.3 g Protein; 7.5 g Net Carb; 1.6 g Fiber;

Ingredients

- 2.65 pounds zucchini, spiralized
- Salt as needed for sprinkling
- 4 tablespoons avocado oil

For the Alfredo Sauce:

- 1 tablespoon minced garlic
- 1 teaspoon salt
- 1 teaspoon ground black pepper, and more for topping
- 1 teaspoon chopped oregano
- 1 tablespoon chopped basil, and more for topping
- ¾ cup butter, unsalted
- 6 ounces Parmesan cheese, grated, and more for topping
- 3 cups heavy cream
- ¾ cup grated cheddar cheese
- 6 ounces cream cheese, softened

Directions

- Prepare the noodles and for this, spiralize zucchini into noodles, place them into a colander, sprinkle with salt and set it aside for 30 minutes or more until zucchini has released its liquid.
- Meanwhile, prepare the sauce and for this, take a medium saucepan, place it over medium heat, add butter and when it melts, add garlic and then cook for 2 minutes until fragrant.
- Then add heavy cream, stir until just mixed, bring it to a simmer, add cream cheese and stir until melted.
- Stir in cheeses in batches until melted, and the smooth sauce comes together, then add remaining ingredients and stir until well combined.

- Remove pan from heat, let the sauce sit until thicken slightly, and then stir it.
- Drain the zoodles and then pat dry them with paper towels.
- Take a large skillet pan, place it over medium-high heat, add oil and when hot, add zucchini noodles, toss until coated with oil and then cook for 2 minutes until softened, don't overcook the noodles.
- Transfer the noodles into a large dish, pour in prepared alfredo sauce, toss until well coated and then sprinkle basil, black pepper, and parmesan cheese on top.
- Serve straight away.

Pasta with Tomato Sauce

Serving: 4

Preparation time: 10 minutes; Cooking time: 12 minutes;

Nutritional Info: 413 Cal; 31.6 g Fats; 28.9 g Protein; 3.1 g Net Carb; 0 g Fiber;

Ingredients

- 4 cups grated mozzarella cheese
- 4 egg yolks
- Tomato sauce, hot, as needed for serving

Directions

- Take a large heatproof bowl, place cheese in it, and then microwave for 5 to 8 minutes until cheese has melted.
- Let the cheese cool for 1 minute and then fold in egg yolks by using a spatula.
- Take a large baking sheet, line it with parchment paper, place cheese mixture on it, cover with another piece of parchment paper of the same manner, and then spread it evenly into a thin dough by using hands.
- Remove the top piece of parchment sheet, cut the dough into thin strips, place the strips on a rack and then refrigerate for a minimum of 4 hours.
- When ready to cook, take a large pot half-full with salty water, bring it to a boil, then add pasta and cook it for 4 minutes.
- Drain the pasta into the colander, run cool water over the pasta, and then distribute evenly among four plates.
- Top the pasta with the tomato sauce and then serve.

Cajun Chicken Pasta

Serving: 3

Preparation time: 5 minutes; Cooking time: 12 minutes;

Nutritional Info: 212 Cal; 11 g Fats; 19 g Protein; 7 g Net Carb; 3 g Fiber;

Ingredients

- 2 chicken breasts, cut into small cubes
- 4 large zucchini, spiralized
- 3 teaspoons Cajun Spice Mix
- 1 tablespoon butter, unsalted
- 1 tablespoon avocado oil
- 1 small green bell pepper, cored, sliced
- 1 small red bell pepper, cored, sliced
- 1 tablespoon minced garlic
- ½ cup heavy cream
- 1 teaspoon salt
- ½ teaspoon ground black pepper

Directions

- Take a medium bowl, place chicken pieces in it, sprinkle with Cajun seasoning, and then toss until well coated.
- Take a large skillet pan, place it over medium-high heat, add butter and oil and when the butter melts, add chicken pieces and then cook for 6 to 7 minutes until cooked and golden brown.
- Switch heat to medium level, add garlic and bell pepper, cook them for 2 minutes until vegetables have turned tender-crisp, then stir until the cream and simmer for 2 minutes.
- Season with salt and black pepper, remove the pan from heat, add zucchini noodles and then toss until well combined.
- Serve straight away.

SOUPS

Coconut Curry Chicken Soup

Serving: 6
Preparation time: 10 minutes; Cooking time: 28 minutes;
Nutritional Info: 223 Cal; 13 g Fats; 17 g Protein; 6 g Net Carb; 2 g Fiber;
Ingredients
- 5 ounces shiitake mushrooms, sliced
- 12 ounces chicken breast, shredded
- ½ cup red pepper, sliced into strips
- 1 tablespoon sliced scallions
- 1 small zucchini, destemmed, cut into half-moons slices
- ½ tablespoon minced garlic
- 2 teaspoons grated ginger
- 2-inch piece of lemongrass
- 1 tablespoon coconut aminos
- 2 tablespoons red curry paste
- 1 lime, juiced, zested
- 1 tablespoon chopped cilantro
- 1 tablespoon butter, unsalted
- 1 tablespoon avocado oil
- 6 cups chicken stock
- 13.5-ounce coconut milk, unsweetened

Directions
- Take a large pot, place it over medium heat, add oil and butter and when the butter melts, add red pepper and mushrooms and then cook for 5 minutes or until saute.
- Add ginger and garlic, stir until mixed, cook for 20 seconds until fragrant, stir in the curry paste, and cook for 10 seconds until toasted.
- Stir in the chicken stock, add chicken, scallions, lemongrass, lime zest, lime juice, and coconut aminos, pour in the milk and let the soup simmer for 15 minutes.
- Add zucchini, cook for 5 minutes until tender, then remove lemongrass and ladle soup into six bowls.
- Garnish the soup with cilantro and then serve.

Chicken Egg Drop Soup

Serving: 4

Preparation time: 5 minutes; Cooking time: 8 minutes;

Nutritional Info: 112 Cal; 6 g Fats; 10 g Protein; 4 g Net Carb; 1 g Fiber;

Ingredients

- 4 medium green onions, sliced
- 8 medium mushrooms, sliced
- 1 teaspoon grated ginger
- 1 ½ teaspoon sea salt
- 1 teaspoon ground black pepper
- 4 eggs
- 4 teaspoons coconut aminos
- 4 cups chicken broth

Directions

- Take a medium saucepan, place it over medium heat, add onion, mushroom, and ginger, stir in black pepper and coconut aminos, pour in the broth, and bring the mixture to a boil.
- Then switch heat to the low level and then simmer the soup for 2 minutes until mushrooms turned tender.
- Take a small bowl, crack eggs in it and then whisk until frothy.
- Stir the egg into the soup in a steady stream and continue stirring until eggs turn into ribbons in the soup.
- Season the soup with salt, then ladle it into four bowls and then serve.

Thai Coconut Soup

Serving: 6

Preparation time: 10 minutes; Cooking time: 40 minutes;

Nutritional Info: 227 Cal; 16 g Fats; 18 g Protein; 3 g Net Carb; 0 g Fiber;

Ingredients

- 4 large chicken breasts, cut into bite-size pieces
- 1 teaspoon ginger powder
- 2 sprigs of Thai basil
- ¼ cup red boat fish sauce
- 2 tablespoons lime juice
- 1 tablespoon coconut aminos
- 2 tablespoons Thai garlic chili paste
- 14 ounces of coconut milk
- 28 ounces of water
- 14 ounces chicken broth
- 6 tablespoons chopped cilantro

Directions

- Take a large pot, place it over high heat, add all the ingredients except for chicken and then stir until mixed.
- Bring the mixture to a boil, add chicken pieces, switch heat to medium-low heat, and then simmer the soap for 30 minutes.
- Remove pot from the heat, discard basil from soup and ladle soup into six bowls.
- Garnish with soup with cilantro and then serve.

SuperFood Keto Soup

Serving: 6

Preparation time: 5 minutes; Cooking time: 25 minutes;

Nutritional Info: 393 Cal; 37.6 g Fats; 5 g Protein; 6.8 g Net Carb; 3 g Fiber;

Ingredients

- 14.1 ounces cauliflower head, cut into small florets
- 7.1 ounces spinach
- 1 medium white onion, peeled, diced
- 5.3 ounces watercress
- 1 tablespoon minced garlic
- 1 ½ teaspoon sea salt
- ¼ teaspoon ground black pepper
- 1 bay leaf, crumbled
- ¼ cup of coconut oil
- 4 cups vegetable stock
- 1 cup coconut milk, unsweetened

Directions

- Take a large pot, place it over medium-high heat, add oil and when it melts, add onion and garlic and then cook for 5 minutes until light brown.
- Add chopped cauliflower florets along with bay leaves, cook for 5 minutes, then add watercress and spinach and continue cooking for 3 minutes or more until leaves have wilted.
- Then pour in the vegetable stock, bring the mixture to a boil, switch heat to medium level, and cook for 7 to 10 minutes until florets have turned tender-crisp.
- Pour in the milk, season soup with salt and black pepper, then remove the pot from heat and puree the soup by using an immersion blender until smooth.
- Serve straight away.

Cheesy Zucchini Soup

Serving: 4

Preparation time: 5 minutes; Cooking time: 20 minutes;

Nutritional Info: 108 Cal; 8 g Fats; 2 g Protein; 4 g Net Carb; 2 g Fiber;

Ingredients

- 3 zucchinis, cut into chunks
- 1 medium onion, peeled, chopped
- ¼ teaspoon ground black pepper
- 1 tablespoon nutritional yeast
- 1 tablespoon chopped parsley
- 2 tablespoons coconut oil
- 1 tablespoon coconut cream
- 2 cups chicken broth

Directions

- Take a medium pot, place it over medium heat, add oil and when it melts, add onion and cook for 5 minutes or until softened.
- Add zucchini, pour in the broth, bring it to a simmer and then cook for 15 minutes until zucchini has cooked through, covering the pot partially.
- When done, stir in yeast, remove the pot from heat and then puree the soup by using an immersion blender until smooth.
- Season the soup with black pepper, garnish with parsley and cream and then serve.

Cheddar and Bacon Soup

Serving: 8
Preparation time: 5 minutes; Cooking time: 30 minutes;
Nutritional Info: 502 Cal; 39.6 g Fats; 32.6 g Protein; 2.75 g Net Carb; 0.25 g Fiber;
Ingredients

- 3 cups cooked chicken, cubed
- ½ cup celery, diced
- ½ of medium white onion, peeled, chopped
- 12 slices of bacon, chopped, cooked
- 1 tablespoon minced garlic
- ¼ teaspoon xanthan gum
- 1 teaspoon salt
- ½ teaspoon cayenne pepper
- ½ teaspoon ground black pepper
- 1 cup heavy whipping cream
- ¼ cup butter, unsalted
- 1 tablespoon avocado oil
- 3 cups shredded cheddar cheese
- 4 cups chicken broth
- 1 tablespoon water

Directions

- Take a large pot, place it over medium heat, add onion and when hot, add celery and onion and then cook for 5 minutes.
- Add butter, wait until it melts, pour in the chicken broth and then bring it to a boil.
- Season the soup with salt, cayenne pepper, and black pepper, stir until mixed, switch heat to medium-low level, and then simmer for 10 minutes.
- Then take a small bowl, stir together water and xanthan gum in it, and stir this mixture into the soup until combined.
- Add cream and cheese and then continue stirring until cheese has melted and blended into the soup.
- Add cooked chicken pieces along with three-fourth of the bacon, stir until mixed and cook for 2 minutes until hot.
- Ladle soup among four bowls, garnish with remaining bacon and more cheese and then serve.

DESSERTS

Wendy's Chocolate Frosty

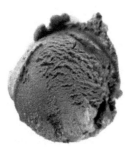

Serving: 2
Preparation time: 10 minutes; Cooking time: 0 minutes;
Nutritional Info: 320 Cal; 34 g Fats; 2 g Protein; 3 g Net Carb; 1 g Fiber;
Ingredients
- ¾ cup heavy whipping cream
- 2 tablespoons Swerve sweetener
- 1 ½ tablespoon cocoa powder, unsweetened
- 1/8 teaspoon salt
- ¾ teaspoon vanilla extract, unsweetened
Directions
- Take a large bowl, add cream in it, then add all the ingredients and whisk by using an immersion blender until stiff peaks form.
- Spoon the mixture into a sealable plastic bag and then place it into the freezer for 35 minutes until frozen.
- When ready to serve, cut a tip of the bag from one corner and then pipe into serving dishes.
- Serve immediately with a spoon.

Wendy's Strawberry Frosty

Serving: 4

Preparation time: 5 minutes; Cooking time: 0 minutes;

Nutritional Info: 215 Cal; 23 g Fats; 1 g Protein; 1 g Net Carb; 0 g Fiber;

Ingredients

- 3 cups heavy whipping cream
- 2 cups whole strawberries, frozen
- 2 scoops of stevia

Directions

- Plug in a food processor, add cream, berries, and stevia and then shut the lid.
- Pulse for 1 to 2 minutes until smooth and then scoop frosty evenly between two bowls.
- Serve immediately with a spoon.

Wendy's Vanilla Frosty

Serving: 4

Preparation time: 5 minutes; Cooking time: 0 minutes;

Nutritional Info: 215 Cal; 23 g Fats; 1 g Protein; 1 g Net Carb; 0 g Fiber;

Ingredients

- 1 cup almond milk, unsweetened
- 4 cups vanilla ice cream, low-carb
- 8 teaspoons Nesquick powder

Directions

- Take a large bowl, add cream in it, then add all the remaining ingredients in it and whisk by using an immersion blender until stiff peaks form.
- Scoop frosty evenly between two bowls and then serve with a spoon.
- Serve immediately.

Krispy Kreme Doughnuts

Serving: 8
Preparation time: 10 minutes; Cooking time: 18 minutes;
Nutritional Info: 74 Cal; 7.5 g Fats; 1 g Protein; 0.7 g Net Carb; 0 g Fiber;
Ingredients
For the Donuts:
- 2 tablespoons whey protein powder, vanilla flavored
- 2 teaspoons baking powder
- 1/8 teaspoon sea salt
- 3 tablespoons erythritol sweetener
- ½ teaspoon stevia powder
- ¾ tablespoon psyllium husk powder
- 2 teaspoons apple cider vinegar
- 2 eggs
- 3 ounces cream cheese, full-fat
- 1 ½ tablespoon butter, unsalted, melted, cooled

For the Frosting:
- 4 ounces mascarpone
- 1 tablespoon swerve confectioners
- 2 teaspoons cocoa powder, unsweetened

Directions
- Switch on the oven, then set it to 150 degrees F and let it preheat.
- Meanwhile, take a large bowl, crack the eggs in it, add salt, both sweeteners, and cream cheese, whisk until blended and then whisk in butter until combined.
- Take a medium bowl, place psyllium husk in it, add whey protein powder, baking powder, and vinegar, stir until combined, and then whisk this mixture into the egg mixture until smooth batter comes together.
- Take two six-donut-molds, scoop its eight molds with the prepared batter in evenly, and then bake for 18 minutes until set and cooked.
- When done, let donuts cool completely in their molds and then lift them out.

- Prepare the frosting and for this, take a medium bowl, place mascarpone in it and then beat until soft peaks form.
- Beat in swerve and cocoa powder until incorporated and then spread the frosting on top of each donut.
- Serve straight away.

Lava Cake

Serving: 4
Preparation time: 10 minutes; Cooking time: 12 minutes;
Nutritional Info: 192 Cal; 15 g Fats; 9 g Protein; 4 g Net Carb; 4 g Fiber;
Ingredients
- 8 tablespoons cocoa powder, unsweetened
- 1 teaspoon baking powder
- 2 teaspoons vanilla extract, unsweetened
- 6 tablespoons erythritol sweetener
- 6 tablespoons heavy whipping cream
- 4 eggs
Directions
- Switch on the oven, then set it to 350 degrees F and let it preheat.
- Meanwhile, take four ramekins, grease them with butter, and set aside until required.
- Take a medium bowl, place cocoa powder in it, add baking powder and erythritol, and then stir until mixed.
- Take a separate medium bowl, crack eggs in it, beat them by using a fork, and then beat in vanilla and cream until blended.
- Beat the egg mixture into the cocoa mixture until incorporated and smooth, then spoon the batter among four ramekins and then bake for 12 minutes until the top of each cake set but still moist.
- When ready to eat, turn each ramekin onto a serving plate and then serve.

Cheesecake Factory Cheesecake

Serving: 8

Preparation time: 15 minutes; Cooking time: 1 hour and 5 minutes;

Nutritional Info: 292 Cal; 25 g Fats; 5.8 g Protein; 10.3 g Net Carb; 0.7 g Fiber;

Ingredients

For the Crust:

- 5 tablespoons butter, unsalted, melted
- 10 graham crackers, low-carb

For the Filling:

- 1 cup swerve sweetener
- 1 teaspoon vanilla extract, unsweetened
- 3 eggs
- 8 ounces cream cheese, softened
- 1 ½ cups water, hot
- 8 ounces sour cream
- Whole strawberries, fresh, for topping

Directions

- Switch on the oven, then set it to 350 degrees F and let it preheat.
- Meanwhile, prepare the crust and for this, place the cracker into a plastic bag, seal it, and then crush the cracker by rolling them with a rolling pin until the mixture resembles sand.
- Tip the mixture into a medium bowl, add melted butter, stir until well combined and then spread the mixture into the bottom of the springform pan.
- Place the pan into the oven, bake the crust for 10 minutes and then let it cool completely.
- While the crust cool, prepare the filling and for this, take a large bowl, place cream cheese in it, and then beat in sweetener until well combined.
- Add vanilla and sour cream, beat until combined and then beat in eggs, one at a time, until blended.

- Wrap the bottom of the cooled springform pan in foil, place it onto a rimmed sheet pan, and then fill the crust with the prepared filling, smooth the top.
- Heat some water until hot, pour it into the sheet pan to make a water bath around the pan, and then bake the cake for 55 minutes until its center is slightly wobbly.
- When done, let the cake cool for 1 hour at room temperature and then cool in the refrigerator for a minimum of 4 hours.
- When ready to eat, use a knife to open up the pan for losing the rim of the pan and then cut out a wedge from the cake.
- Serve the cake with berries.

DRINKS

Starbucks Pink Drink

Serving: 2
Preparation time: 5 minutes; Cooking time: 0 minutes;
Nutritional Info: 379 Cal; 21 g Fats; 2 g Protein; 4 g Net Carb; 0 g Fiber;
Ingredients
- 2 cups passion tea, brewed, cooled
- ½ cup heavy cream
- 2 tablespoons vanilla syrup, sugar-free
- 1 ½ cup ice cubes
Directions
- Add all the ingredients in the order into a food processor except for ice, shut with the lid, and then pulse for 1 minute until smooth.
- Divide the ice cubes evenly between two glasses, pour in the drink, and then serve.

Starbucks Iced Matcha Latte

Serving: 2

Preparation time: 5 minutes; Cooking time: 0 minutes;

Nutritional Info: 199 Cal; 16.1 g Fats; 5 g Protein; 4 g Net Carb; 4.5 g Fiber;

Ingredients

- 2 cups almond milk, unsweetened
- 2 tablespoons vanilla syrup, sugar-free
- 2 tablespoons avocado oil
- 2 teaspoons matcha powder
- 2 cups of ice cubes

Directions

- Add all the ingredients in the order into a food processor except for ice, shut with the lid, and then pulse for 1 minute until smooth.
- Divide the ice cubes evenly between two glasses, pour in the latte, and then serve.

Starbucks Coffee Frappuccino

Serving: 2

Preparation time: 5 minutes; Cooking time: 0 minutes;

Nutritional Info: 182 Cal; 14.7 g Fats; 1 g Protein; 0.5 g Net Carb; 0.6 g Fiber;

Ingredients

- ½ cup heavy cream
- ½ cup strong coffee, brewed, cooled
- ¾ tablespoons erythritol sweetener
- 3 tablespoons caramel sauce, low-carb
- 1 ½ cups ice cubes
- 1/4 cup whipping cream

Directions

- Add all the ingredients in the order into a food processor except for whipping cream, shut with the lid, and then pulse for 1 minute until smooth.
- Divide the drink evenly between two glasses, top with the whipped cream, and then serve.

Starbucks Pumpkin Spice Frappuccino

Serving: 2

Preparation time: 5 minutes; Cooking time: 0 minutes;

Nutritional Info: 263.5 Cal; 23.4 g Fats; 3.3 g Protein; 7.7 g Net Carb; 2.2 g Fiber;

Ingredients

- 2/3 cup almond milk, vanilla flavored, unsweetened
- 2/3 cup pumpkin puree
- 2/3 cup coconut milk, unsweetened
- 1 ½ teaspoon pumpkin pie spice and more for topping
- 1 teaspoon vanilla extract, unsweetened
- 2 teaspoons liquid stevia
- 4 teaspoons instant coffee granules
- 2 cups of ice cubes
- ½ cup whipped coconut cream

Directions

- Add all the ingredients in the order into a food processor except for whipped cream, shut with the lid, and then pulse for 1 minute until smooth.
- Divide the drink evenly between two glasses, top with the whipped cream, sprinkle with pumpkin pie spice, and then serve.

Starbucks Peppermint Mocha Coffee

Serving: 2

Preparation time: 5 minutes; Cooking time: 2 minutes;

Nutritional Info: 197 Cal; 19 g Fats; 1 g Protein; 2.4 g Net Carb; 2.8 g Fiber;

Ingredients

- 2 cups almond milk, unsweetened
- 1 cup brewed coffee, cooled
- 4 tablespoons heavy whipping cream
- ½ teaspoon peppermint extract, unsweetened
- 2 tablespoons cocoa powder
- 6 tablespoons Swerve Confectioners
- 2 tablespoons MCT Oil Powder, Chocolate flavored
- ½ cup whipped cream
- 2 teaspoons chocolate shavings, low-carb

Directions

- Add all the ingredients in the order into a food processor except for whipped cream, peppermint extract, and chocolate shavings, shut with the lid, and then pulse for 1 minute until smooth.
- Pour the mixture into a medium pan, place it over medium heat and cook for 2 minutes until warm.
- Remove the pan from heat, add peppermint extract and then stir until mixed.
- Divide the drink evenly between two glasses, top with whipped cream, sprinkle with chocolate shavings, and then serve.

Vanilla Bean Frappuccino

Serving: 2

Preparation time: 5 minutes; Cooking time: 0 minutes;

Nutritional Info: 217 Cal; 23 g Fats; 1 g Protein; 2 g Net Carb; 0 g Fiber;

Ingredients

- ½ cup heavy whipping cream
- 1 cups vanilla almond milk, unsweetened
- ½ teaspoon liquid stevia, vanilla flavored
- ½ of vanilla bean, split lengthwise, inside scraped out
- ½ cup whipped cream
- 1 cup of ice cubes
- 2 teaspoons chocolate shavings, low-carb

Directions

- Add all the ingredients in the order into a food processor except for whipped cream, ice, and chocolate shavings, shut with the lid, and then pulse for 1 minute until smooth.
- Add ice and then continue blending for 30 seconds until the ice has crushed
- Divide the drink evenly between two glasses, top with the whipped cream, sprinkle with chocolate shavings, and then serve.

Irish Cream Liqueur

Serving: 12
Preparation time: 5 minutes; Cooking time: 7 minutes;
Nutritional Info: 138 Cal; 14.1 g Fats; 1.4 g Protein; 1.5 g Net Carb; 0.3 g Fiber;
Ingredients
- 1 teaspoon vanilla extract, unsweetened
- 1 tablespoon cocoa powder
- 2/3 cup erythritol sweetener
- 1 teaspoon almond extract, unsweetened
- 1 teaspoon instant coffee
- 1 1/3 cups Irish whiskey
- 2 cups heavy cream

Directions
- Take a small saucepan, place it over medium heat, add cream and erythritol, whisk well and then cook for 3 minutes until sweetener has dissolved.
- Then add coffee, cocoa powder, both extracts, whisk well until well combined and then remove the pan from heat.
- Pour in whiskey, stir until well combined, pour the mixture into an air-tight jar, cover with the lid and let it chill in the refrigerator until ready to use,

Chick-fil-A Frozen Lemonade

Serving: 2

Preparation time: 5 minutes; Cooking time: 0 minutes;

Nutritional Info: 546 Cal; 45.5 g Fats; 5.5 g Protein; 28 g Net Carb; 5.5 g Fiber;

Ingredients

- 1 packet lemonade mix, sugar-free
- 2 cups vanilla ice cream, sugar-free
- ¼ cup lemon juice
- 1 cup of water

Directions

- Add all the ingredients in the order into a food processor except ice cream, shut with the lid, and then pulse for 10 seconds until smooth.
- Add ice cream and then continue blending for 10 seconds until the drink reaches to desired consistency.
- Divide the lemonade between two glasses and then serve.

Starbucks White Drink

Serving: 2
Preparation time: 5 minutes; Cooking time: 0 minutes;
Nutritional Info: 168 Cal; 18 g Fats; 2 g Protein; 4 g Net Carb; 0 g Fiber;
Ingredients
- 1 teaspoon vanilla extract, unsweetened
- 1 cup peach white tea, brewed
- ½ cup whipped coconut cream
- 2/3 cup coconut cream
- 1 cup of ice cubes

Directions
- Add all the ingredients in the order into a food processor except whipped cream, shut with the lid, and then pulse for 30 seconds until smooth.
- Divide the drink between two glasses, top evenly with whipped cream and then serve.

SAUCES AND DRESSINGS

Chick-Fil-A Sauce

Serving: 4
Preparation time: 5 minutes; Cooking time: 0 minutes;
Nutritional Info: 183 Cal; 20 g Fats; 0 g Protein; 0 g Net Carb; 0 g Fiber;
Ingredients
- ¼ teaspoon onion powder
- ¼ teaspoon garlic salt
- ½ tablespoon yellow mustard
- ¼ teaspoon smoked paprika
- ½ tablespoon stevia extract, powdered
- 1 teaspoon liquid smoke
- ½ cup mayonnaise
Directions
- Plug in a food processor, add all the ingredients in it, cover with the lid and then pulse for 30 seconds until smooth.
- Tip the sauce into a bowl and then serve.

Burger Sauce

Serving: 12
Preparation time: 5 minutes; Cooking time: 0 minutes;
Nutritional Info: 15 Cal; 7 g Fats; 0 g Protein; 0 g Net Carb; 0 g Fiber;
Ingredients
- 1 tablespoon chopped gherkin
- ½ teaspoon chopped dill
- ¾ teaspoon onion powder
- ¾ teaspoon garlic powder
- 1/8 teaspoon ground white pepper
- 1 teaspoon mustard powder
- ½ teaspoon erythritol sweetener
- ¼ teaspoon sweet paprika
- 1 teaspoon white vinegar
- ½ cup mayonnaise

Directions
- Take a medium bowl, place all the ingredients for the sauce in it and then stir until well mixed.
- Place the sauce for a minimum of overnight in the refrigerator to develop flavors and then serve with burgers.

Pollo Tropical's Curry Mustard Sauce

Serving: 12

Preparation time: 5 minutes; Cooking time: 0 minutes;

Nutritional Info: 66 Cal; 7 g Fats; 1 g Protein; 0 g Net Carb; 1 g Fiber;

Ingredients

- 2 teaspoon curry powder
- 4 teaspoons mustard paste
- 8 tablespoons mayonnaise

Directions

- Plug in a food processor, add all the ingredients in it, cover with the lid and then pulse for 30 seconds until smooth.
- Tip the sauce into a bowl and then serve.

El Fenix Chili Gravy

Serving: 28
Preparation time: 5 minutes; Cooking time: 40 minutes;
Nutritional Info: 22 Cal; 2 g Fats; 0 g Protein; 0 g Net Carb; 0 g Fiber;
Ingredients
- 2 tablespoons coconut flour
- ½ teaspoon salt
- ½ teaspoon ground black pepper
- 1/2 teaspoon dried Mexican oregano leaves
- 1 ½ teaspoon garlic powder
- 2 teaspoons ground cumin
- ½ teaspoon ground coriander
- 2 tablespoons oat fiber
- 2 tablespoons red chili powder
- 1/8 teaspoon dried thyme leaves
- ¼ cup lard
- 2 cups beef broth
Directions
- Take a medium skillet pan, place it over medium heat, add lard and when it melts, stir in flour, and then cook for 3 to 5 minutes until nicely browned, frequently lifting the pan from heat to cool slightly and then bring it back onto the fire.
- Stir in oat fiber, garlic, thyme, oregano, cumin, and coriander until mixed and cook for 2 minutes until it gets thick, stirring constantly.
- Then whisk in the broth until smooth, switch heat to the low level, and simmer the gravy fo3 30 minutes until sauce thickens.
- Remove pan from heat and serve.

Sweet and Smoky Chipotle Vinaigrette

Serving: 32

Preparation time: 5 minutes; Cooking time: 0 minutes;

Nutritional Info: 103 Cal; 11.5 g Fats; 0.05 g Protein; 3.05 g Net Carb; 0.05 g Fiber;

Ingredients

- 1 teaspoon garlic powder
- 1 teaspoon cumin
- 1 tablespoon salt
- 1 ½ tablespoon ground black pepper
- 1 teaspoon oregano leaves
- 1/3 cup liquid stevia
- ½ cup red wine vinegar
- 1 ½ cups avocado oil
- 1 tablespoon adobo sauce
- 1 tablespoon water

Directions

- Plug in a food processor, add all the ingredients in it except for oil, cover with the lid and then pulse for 30 seconds until smooth.
- Blend in oil in a steady stream until emulsified and then pour the salad dressing into a medium bowl.
- Serve straight away.

Bang Bang Sauce

Serving: 6
Preparation time: 5 minutes; Cooking time: 0 minutes;
Nutritional Info: 90 Cal; 10 g Fats; 0 g Protein; 1 g Net Carb; 0 g Fiber;
Ingredients
- ¼ cup mayonnaise
- 1 ½ tablespoon garlic chili sauce
- 1 tablespoon rice vinegar
- 2 tablespoons monk fruit Sweetener
- 1/8 teaspoon salt

Directions
- Plug in a food processor, add all the ingredients in it, cover with the lid and then pulse for 30 seconds until smooth.
- Tip the sauce into a bowl and then serve.

Sweet Chili Sauce

Serving: 6
Preparation time: 5 minutes; Cooking time: 15 minutes;
Nutritional Info: 25 Cal; 2.2 g Fats; 0 g Protein; 1.2 g Net Carb; 0 g Fiber;
Ingredients
- 1 tablespoon garlic chili sauce
- ½ cup of water
- 2 scoops of beef bone broth collagen
- ¼ cup unseasoned rice vinegar
- 1 ½ teaspoon minced garlic
- ¼ teaspoon ground ginger
- ¼ cup erythritol sweetener
- 1 tablespoon avocado oil
Directions
- Take a large bowl, place all the ingredients in it except for oil and then whisk well until well combined.
- Take a medium saucepan, place it over medium heat, add sauce mixture and then simmer it for 15 minutes until the sauce has thickened.
- When done, remove the pan from heat, stir in oil, let the sauce cool completely and then serve.

Big Mac Sauce

Serving: 6

Preparation time: 5 minutes; Cooking time: minutes;

Nutritional Info: 138 Cal; 16 g Fats; 0 g Protein; 1 g Net Carb; 0.1 g Fiber;

Ingredients

- 1 tablespoon diced white onion
- 2 tablespoons diced pickles
- 1 teaspoon erythritol sweetener
- 1 tablespoon ketchup, low-carb
- 1 teaspoon dill pickle juice
- ½ cup mayonnaise

Directions

- Take a small bowl, place all of its ingredients in it and then stir well until incorporated.
- Serve straight away or store the sauce in an air-tight container.

Caramel Sauce

Serving: 12
Preparation time: 5 minutes; Cooking time: 15 minutes;
Nutritional Info: 91 Cal; 10 g Fats; 1 g Protein; 0 g Net Carb; 1 g Fiber;
Ingredients
- 3 tablespoons erythritol sweetener
- 1 teaspoon vanilla extract, unsweetened
- 1/3 cup butter, salted
- 2/3 cup heavy cream

Directions
- Take a medium saucepan, place it over low heat, add butter and erythritol and then cook for 4 to 5 minutes until butter melts and turn golden brown.
- Stir in cream, bring it to a gentle boil and then simmer the sauce for 10 minutes until the sauce has thickened to coat the back of the spoon, stirring constantly.
- Remove pan from heat, stir in vanilla extract and then serve.

Paula Deen BBQ Sauce

Serving: 32

Preparation time: 5 minutes; Cooking time: 5 minutes;

Nutritional Info: 10 Cal; 2 g Fats; 0 g Protein; 2 g Net Carb; 0 g Fiber;

Ingredients

- 1 teaspoon onion powder
- 1 teaspoon salt
- ½ teaspoon cayenne pepper
- 1 teaspoon ground black pepper
- ¾ cup erythritol sweetener
- 2 teaspoons paprika
- ½ teaspoon cinnamon
- 2 tablespoons mustard paste
- ½ teaspoon xanthan gum
- 3 tablespoons lemon juice
- 1 ½ tablespoons liquid smoke
- ½ cup apple cider vinegar
- ¾ cup ketchup, low-carb
- 1 tablespoon Worcestershire sauce
- ½ cup of water

Directions

- Take a medium saucepan, place it over medium heat, add mustard, Worcestershire sauce, liquid smoke, and ketchup in it, and then pour in vinegar, lemon juice, and water.
- Whisk until combined, cook it for 3 to 4 minutes until sauce begins to bubbles, and then whisk in xanthan gum until incorporated.
- Then add erythritol and all the spices, whisk until combined, and remove the pan from heat.
- Let the sauce cool completely, then serve immediately or store it in an air-tight jar or squeeze bottle.

Chorizo Queso Fundido

Serving: 6

Preparation time: 5 minutes; Cooking time: 25 minutes;

Nutritional Info: 402 Cal; 33 g Fats; 22 g Protein; 4 g Net Carb; 1 g Fiber;

Ingredients

- 8 ounces Mexican chorizo
- 1 Roma tomato, cored, seeded and diced
- 2 tablespoons minced garlic
- 1/2 of a large onion, peeled, sliced
- 1 roasted poblano pepper, seeded, cut into strips
- ½ teaspoon of sea salt
- 2 cups shredded Monterey Jack Cheese
- 1 cup Mexican cream

Directions

- Take a large skillet pan, place it over medium heat, add chorizo, break it up and then cook for 10 to 12 minutes until nicely brown and crisp.
- When done, drain excess grease, transfer chorizo to a bowl, and then set it aside until required.
- Return pan over medium heat, add onion and then cook it for 5 minutes until tender.
- Add tomato, pepper strips and garlic, season with salt, cook the mixture for 2 minutes until hot and then spoon the mixture into the bowl containing chorizo.
- Remove skillet pan from the heat, pour in cream and cheese, and then blend for 5 minutes or more until cheese has melted.
- Return the skillet pan over medium heat, add half of the chorizo mixture, stir until mixed and cook for 5 minutes until creamy.
- Top it with the remaining chorizo mixture, place the pan under the broiler and cook for 3 minutes until the mixture begins to bubble.
- Serve it with low-carb tortilla chips.

Alfredo Sauce

Serving: 6

Preparation time: 5 minutes; Cooking time: 10 minutes;

Nutritional Info: 531 Cal; 53.8 g Fats; 10.3 g Protein; 3.7 g Net Carb; 0.1 g Fiber;

Ingredients

- 1 tablespoon minced garlic
- 1/8 teaspoon salt
- 1/8 teaspoon ground white pepper
- 1/8 teaspoon ground nutmeg
- 1 ½ cups grated Parmesan cheese
- 2 cups heavy whipping cream
- ½ cup butter, unsalted
- 2 ounces cream cheese, softened

Directions

- Take a medium saucepan, place it over medium heat, add butter and when it melts, add garlic and then cook for 2 minutes until fragrant.
- Then add cream cheese and heavy cream, stir until just mixed and stir in parmesan until melted.
- Cook the sauce for 5 to 7 minutes until sauce thickens to the desired level and then stir in salt, white pepper, and nutmeg.
- Serve straight away.

VEGETABLES

Coleslaw

Serving: 6

Preparation time: 5 minutes; Cooking time: 0 minutes;

Nutritional Info: 205 Cal; 20 g Fats; 1 g Protein; 2 g Net Carb; 2 g Fiber;

Ingredients

- 14 ounces coleslaw mix
- 3 tablespoons erythritol sweetener
- ½ teaspoon celery salt
- ½ teaspoon ground black pepper
- 1 tablespoon apple cider vinegar
- 1 ½ tablespoon lemon juice
- 1 teaspoon mustard paste
- ¾ cup mayonnaise

Directions

- Take a large bowl, add all the ingredients in it except for coleslaw mix and then whisk until smooth.
- Add coleslaw mix, stir until well combined, and then taste to adjust the seasoning.
- Serve straight away.

Zesty Zucchini Chips

Serving: 4

Preparation time: 10 minutes; Cooking time: 1 hour and 5 minutes;

Nutritional Info: 62 Cal; 7 g Fats; 0.2 g Protein; 0.2 g Net Carb; 0 g Fiber;

Ingredients

- 2 medium zucchini, ends trimmed
- 1 teaspoon of sea salt
- 2 tablespoons avocado oil

Directions

- Switch on the oven, then set it to 250 degrees F and let it preheat.
- Meanwhile, prepare the chips, and for this, cut them into thin slices.
- Take a baking sheet, line it with paper towels, spread zucchini slices in a single layer, sprinkle with salt, and then let them sit for 10 minutes.
- After 10 minutes, remove excess liquid from zucchini and then spread zucchini slices to a baking sheet lined with parchment paper.
- Brush the zucchini slices with oil and then bake for 45 to 65 minutes until crisp and nicely golden, turning halfway.
- When done, let chips cool for 5 minutes and then serve with dip.

Fauxtato Chips

Serving: 4

Preparation time: 10 minutes; Cooking time: 1 hour and 15 minutes;

Nutritional Info: 32 Cal; 3.4 g Fats; 0.1 g Protein; 0.1 g Net Carb; 0.1 g Fiber;

Ingredients

- 7 medium radishes, peeled, thinly sliced
- ½ teaspoon garlic powder
- 1 ½ teaspoon salt
- ¾ teaspoon ground black pepper
- 1 tablespoon avocado oil

Directions

- Switch on the oven, then set it to 225 degrees F and let it preheat.
- Prepare the radish and for this, peel them, cut them into thin slices, and then place the slices in a large bowl.
- Add garlic powder, salt, black pepper, and oil, toss until coated and then spread the radish slices in a single layer on a large baking sheet.
- Bake the radish chips for 1 hour and 15 minutes until crisp and nicely golden, turning halfway.
- When done, let chips cool for 5 minutes and then serve with dip.

Vegetarian Pizza

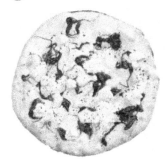

Serving: 8

Preparation time: 10 minutes; Cooking time: 20 minutes;

Nutritional Info: 44 Cal; 4 g Fats; 1 g Protein; 1 g Net Carb; 0.2 g Fiber;

Ingredients

- ½ cup baby spinach
- 1 cauliflower crust
- 1 tablespoon avocado oil

Directions

- Switch on the oven, then set it to 425 degrees F and let it preheat.
- Meanwhile, prepare the crust as instructed on its packet and then place it over a baking sheet or pizza pan.
- Drizzle oil over the crust, spread the spinach on top and then bake for 20 minutes until the crust turns nicely brown.
- When done, let the pizza cool for 5 minutes, then cut it into eight wedges and serve.

Mac and Cheese

Serving: 6

Preparation time: 10 minutes; Cooking time: 35 minutes;

Nutritional Info: 316.8 Cal; 26.8 g Fats; 10.3 g Protein; 6 g Net Carb; 2.8 g Fiber;

Ingredients

- 1 large head of cauliflower
- 1/8 teaspoon garlic powder
- ½ teaspoon salt
- ¼ teaspoon ground black pepper
- 1 ½ teaspoons mustard paste
- 2 ounces cream cheese, cut into small pieces
- 1 ½ cup shredded cheddar cheese, divided
- 1 cup heavy cream

Directions

- Cut the cauliflower head into small florets, place them in a large heatproof bowl, and then it with a plastic wrap.
- Place the bowl into the microwave oven and then heat to for 10 to 15 minutes until florets have turned tender-crisp.
- Meanwhile, take a medium baking dish and grease it with oil.
- Drain the cauliflower florets, pat dry with paper towels and then transfer them into the prepared baking dish.
- Prepare the sauce and for this, take a small saucepan, place it over medium heat, add cream and then bring it to a simmer.
- Whisk in mustard and cream cheese until smooth, stir in garlic powder, salt, black pepper, and 1 cup of cheddar cheese and whisk well until the cheese has melted.
- Pour the sauce over cauliflower florets, spread remaining cheese on top and then bake for 15 minutes until the mixture bubbles and the top turns golden brown.
- When done, let mac and cheese cool for 5 minutes and then serve.

9 781649 844125